12 Steps on Buddha's Path

Steps on Buddha's Path

12 Steps on Buddha's Path

Bill, Buddha, and We

A SPIRITUAL JOURNEY
OF RECOVERY

LAURA S.

Wisdom Publications, Inc.
199 Elm Street
Somerville MA 02144 USA
wisdomexperience.org

Library of Congress Cataloging-in-Publication Data

S., Laura.
12 steps on Buddha's path : Bill, Buddha, and we : a spiritual journey
of recovery / Laura S.
p. cm.
Includes index.
ISBN 0-86171-281-1 (pbk. : alk. paper)
1. Twelve-step programs—Religious aspects—Buddhism. 2. Religious
life—Buddhism. 3. Alcoholics—Religious life. 4. Alcoholism—Religious
aspects—Buddhism.   I. Title. II. Title: Twelve steps on Buddha's
path.
BQ4570.T85S7 2006
294.3'3762292—dc22

2005034846

ISBN 978-0-86171-281-6
eBook ISBN 978-0-86171-993-8

24 23 22 21
9   8   7   6

Cover design by Laura Shaw.
Interior design by DCDesign, Inc. Set in Goudy 11.5/17 pt.

Wisdom Publications' books are printed on acid-free paper and meet the
guidelines for permanence and durability set by the Council of Library
Resources.

Printed in the United States of America.

MAY ALL BEINGS

BE WELL, HAPPY, AND FREE,

ONE STEP AT A TIME,

ONE MOMENT AT A TIME.

CONTENTS

PART TWO: BUDDHA

PART THREE: WE

FOREWORD

I OFTEN HAVE the opportunity to speak about the benefits of my Buddhist meditation practice to groups of people who have no background in Buddhism. It might be at the monthly meeting of the Parent / Teacher Association of the local middle school, the Library Club of a senior residential center, the Tuesday morning breakfast meeting of the Rotary Club in a nearby town, or the spring benefit luncheon of the county Association of Family Lawyers. The ages of the people in the audience vary and their reasons for coming together are different, but my message is basically the same wherever I go:

I tell them that the Buddha taught meditations as one way of cultivating wisdom and kindness. I say that the fundamental premise behind all the practices that the Buddha taught is that it is possible to have minds that are peaceful in the middle of lives, and in the middle of a world, that are continually and inevitably problematic.

I begin with the first of the Four Noble Truths, the Buddha's summary expression of his understanding of the causes and the end of suffering. Life is difficult, he taught, inherently challenging, because it requires constant accommodation to changing, often painful, circumstances. I say the Second Noble Truth this way: Suffering is the insatiable need to have things be other than what they are. I continue with the Third Noble Truth: Peace is possible, happiness is possible, because peace and happiness in life do not depend on what is going on but rather on how the heart and mind respond to what is happening. I add that the Fourth Noble Truth is the program of practices the Buddha taught to promote the heart's wise response.

It is very often at this point that someone in the audience will say, "Wait a minute. I say something like this every day. I say, 'God, grant me the serenity to accept the things I cannot change, the courage to change the things I can change, and the wisdom to know the difference.' Isn't that what you're saying?"

I say, "Yes. It is."

The idiom of the 2,500-year-old Buddhist tradition and the idiom of contemporary Twelve Step teachings are different, but both paths share the powerful message of the possibility of peace and happiness. The author of this book has used her own experience in decades of Twelve Step work and as a Buddhist meditator as the vehicle for presenting both practice paths. As I read these parallel reflections, echoing the promise of the end of suffering back and forth between them, the promise of liberation from suffering sounded stronger and stronger, as if two familiar voices were calling out "*Yes!*" and "*Amen!*" to each other. I finished the book inspired. It renewed my zeal. I think it will do the same for you.

The author, writing under the pseudonym Laura S., offers this book anonymously, in respect to the Twelve Step commitment to anonymity and in the understanding that no one does anything alone. Everything anyone does is an expression of all the circumstances, connections, and communities that have been part of that person's experience. Laura S., Bill W., the Buddha, and We all wrote this book. May all of us and all beings share in its merit.

SYLVIA BOORSTEIN

PREFACE

ON MY THIRTY-THIRD birthday I swallowed a bottleful of sleeping pills and died: in the ambulance to the hospital, I stopped breathing and my heart stopped beating.

No one who knew me could comprehend what had driven the person they saw as an intelligent, attractive, successful business-woman to such a desperate act. On the outside, everything about my life looked rich; inside, I was emotionally and spiritually bank-rupt. I woke up every morning crying because I was still alive. I was in unbearable emotional pain and I couldn't imagine that anything would ever change. I just had to hang on as long as I could, then find a way to end the pain—and me. In the next two years I made two other serious suicide attempts, spent time in locked wards of mental hospitals, and lost all the things that had made my life look good on the outside—career, partner, home, car, sailboat, and above all, my heavily defended façade. I was broke and broken.

After I lost everything that propped up my façade, I was able to cut through my denial, one of the most pervasive characteristics of the disease of alcoholism, and come face to face with the fact that I was a drunk and that the "medicine" I took to get through my life was fueling the depression that almost ended it. Destitute and unable to work, I was brought to my knees and then I reached out for help. I did what until then had been unimaginable: I went to Alcoholics Anonymous. There I was surrounded by people who told me that they knew how I felt, and I knew that they did because they too had been trapped in the despair-filled cycle of alcoholism, and I let them love me back to life.

Slowly, fighting the desire to drink again, sometimes fighting the program that was helping me not give in to that compulsion, I eventually experienced "rebirth": a new life unlike any I could have imagined. My struggle with the disease of alcoholism as I began my spiritual journey in Alcoholics Anonymous is portrayed in Part One of this book. As rewarding as my recovery was, I still found myself in a spiritual search for something to fill the black hole inside that was smaller but still there. Much to my surprise, because I had intellectually rejected it as a teenager, I found what I was looking for in Buddhism. As the result of some extraordinary experiences in the Himalayas, that attraction to Buddhism finally made the crucial twelve-inch drop from my head to my heart, a passage described in Part Two.

When I started out in AA, I thought I could carefully read the Twelve Steps and master the program of recovery. When I began to investigate Buddhism, I thought I could thoroughly study the Four Noble Truths and master the teachings of the Buddha. I was wrong in both cases. For me, the process has been something like nurturing an orchid seedpod, which takes seven years to bloom. If a seedpod is from an existing, well-established species, we can anticipate what its flower will look like—just as we can see around us examples of what recovery is like for someone in AA or how practice transforms someone who is a Buddhist. But if we're creating an orchid hybrid, we have no idea what we're going to get at the end of the seven years. It may look as if nothing is happening to the seedpod for years, but on the inside rare beauty is being created if we continuously nurture the seedpod and our own faith.

In AA I was never asked to take anything on blind faith—I was urged to find evidence among other recovering alcoholics for everything I was asked to believe. So too had the Buddha repeatedly told his adherents not to accept anything he taught without testing out its truth for themselves. What was common to AA and Buddhism was the idea that if I do what I did (surrender to my attachment to alcohol or anything else), I'll get what I got (great suffering); but if I do what liberated beings do, I'll get what they got—in the case of alcoholism, a recovery that is happy, joyous, and free. In both cases, it helped me enormously that rather than some authority figure telling me what to do, there were wise beings who had achieved what I wanted and were telling me what they had done. If I wanted to be a joyfully recovering alcoholic, all I had to do was follow in the footsteps of those who had climbed the Twelve Steps before me. If I wanted to be a bodhisattva ("enlightenment being"), all I had to do was walk in the footsteps of those who had mindfully followed the Buddha's Eightfold Path.

AA and Buddhism became inextricably linked for me when I began to seriously study the Four Noble Truths, and the flowering of that hybrid is described in Part Three. What first erupted into my awareness was the obvious truth that all forms of addiction are dukkha (the Pali word for "suffering"). I also realized that all dukkha is a form of addiction to something—perhaps to a sensual pleasure, a person, an object, or even life itself. When I was imprisoned by alcoholism, I was not free, nor did I believe that I had choices. Imprisoned by dukkha, I was powerless.

My first "miracle" in AA was learning that I do have choices—as long as I do not pick up the first drink—and even that I have a choice whether to pick it up. In Buddhist terms, I encountered the "law of karma," which states simply that every *intentional action* (the definition of *karma*) will produce an effect when the right conditions arise. I gained the crucial understanding that I can't change my past karma—my past intentions, my past actions, and their accumulated results—but I can change my future karma if I am mindfully making choices in the present. In AA terms, if I don't pick up a drink, I won't get drunk. It was the same lesson from different perspectives.

ABOUT ANONYMITY

In addition to the familiar Twelve Steps, AA also has the lesser known Twelve Traditions (see the Appendix), which are excellent guidelines for AA groups, just as the steps are for individuals. The Twelve Traditions have also been very helpful to my personal recovery, especially the twelfth, which states: "Anonymity is the spiritual foundation of all our traditions, ever reminding us to place principles above personalities" (*Twelve Steps and Twelve Traditions*, p. 184). Unfortunately, far too many famous "personalities" have exploited their sobriety through AA by self-aggrandizement, taking all the credit for themselves in some cases or—well-meaning but misguided—trying to "promote" AA by telling how it has changed their lives. All too often, these people in the spotlight have picked up drinking again, giving themselves and Alcoholics Anonymous a black eye. Many struggling alcoholics who are resistant to going to AA and repeatedly have relapses excuse their own "slips" by pointing to these well-known people and saying, "You see? AA doesn't work." Reading tabloid headlines may give a relapser the rationalization to stay away from AA, and the miracle of recovery may never happen for her or him.

Anonymity is also a priceless gift for newcomers to AA. Most of us have a fairly high shame quotient—and in some cases are legally vulnerable for our past actions—and we need for AA to be a safe place for us to share aloud whatever may be threatening our sobriety if we choose to. The guideline is that each of us can tell another individual (but not at the level of print, film, video, or other media) that we are in AA, but we may not break the anonymity of another person.

Anonymity, for each of us personally, is the basis of humility in recovery: Only through our anonymity can we give credit where credit is due: to all those drunks who have gotten sober and stayed sober before us. Through anonymity, all us garden-variety alcoholics become a *We* instead of an *I* and know the blessing of joining the human race in sobriety. Out of respect for the tradition of anonymity I have used the pen name "Laura S." and have avoided using the real names of other people in AA.

OTHER TWELVE
STEP PROGRAMS

For more than seventy years, the success of Alcoholics Anonymous in helping supposedly hopeless drunks to recover has inspired the founding of other Twelve Step programs for people addicted to a wide variety of substances and behaviors, and other programs for the people who love someone in recovery. The first of these "other As," now called Al-Anon Family Groups, was established by Lois W., AA cofounder Bill W.'s wife, during the earliest days of Alcoholics Anonymous. While Bill and other drunks met in their living room, Lois and the others' wives (all the earliest members were men) sat around the kitchen table exploring the emotional devastation *they* had experienced as the result of the disease of alcoholism in someone they loved. As Al-Anon took shape and name in later years, it relied heavily on the Twelve Steps of AA for its program of recovery, as has Ala-Teen, a program for young people affected by the drinking of their parents or other adults. Since those early days, it seems as if as many organizations as there are addictions have arisen: Narcotics Anonymous, Overeaters Anonymous, Gamblers Anonymous, Sex Addicts Anonymous—the list goes on and on. All of these organizations have based their recovery programs on AA's Twelve Steps—modified only slightly in some cases, changed greatly in others.

I have often been asked to speak at such meetings, especially about the Twelve Steps. So although this book describes my recovery from alcoholism, the discussions of the steps and other parts of AA's program can easily be used by anyone in any other Twelve Step program.

As AAs love to say, the steps work if you work them—for a remarkably wide range of recoveries.

My journey through recovery has been an astonishing passage through strange and frightening territory, but it has made me joyous and free, as well as the kind of wise and compassionate person I always wanted to be. The hybrid of AA and Buddhism has been more beautiful and enriching than anything I could have ever imagined. I'm so pleased that you're joining me for some steps on its path.

LAURA S.

Part One:
Bill W.

"I am an alcoholic."

HAS IT COME
TO THIS?

I WALKED DOWN Hudson Street until I reached the corner. I stopped and looked up at the street sign: Bank Street. I checked my watch: 6:55 PM. I opened the notebook to see where I was supposed to be going: "St. Luke's in the Village, where Grove Street intersects Hudson." I moved on to the next corner and read the sign: West 11th Street. It was 6:59 PM. Forty-three electroshock "treatments" had left my mind so porous that I had to go through this agenda at every corner in order to reach St. Luke's for the Monday night AA Beginner's Meeting, seven blocks from my apartment in New York City.

I recently had signed myself out of one of New England's most prestigious hospitals—highly esteemed, but highly ignorant about alcoholism. When the gurney wheeled me into the emergency room after yet another suicide attempt, the medical staff fought for my life. No one, including my closest friends, could understand why I wanted to die so much that I would swallow a bottle of sleeping pills or slash my wrists, which I had done in another attempt. So the hospital psychiatric staff did the only thing they knew to do for "severe depression": they fried my brains with electroconvulsive "therapy" (ECT), leaving me with permanently impaired memory as well as the original depression that I now know was incubated within the disease of alcoholism. But none of my "friends" ever questioned my drinking. I was too intelligent and accomplished to be an alcoholic—wasn't I?—to fit their stereotype of a drunk stumbling down the street in the Bowery. And if they wondered about my drinking, they'd have to look at their own, because I always hung out with people who drank at least as much as I did.

So I slithered into St. Luke's—peeking out from under a large floppy hat that almost met my upturned collar. I was in disguise. I had taken a seat in the back of the room before I realized there was a coffee urn, and I didn't want to get up again, because someone might guess that I hadn't known the meeting had coffee and was a newcomer. Besides, my hand was shaking too much to hold a cup without splashing the coffee. I was like a teenager again, self-consciously sure that everyone was looking at me. When the meeting started, people turned their attention to a man in the front of the room reading something called the AA Preamble, so I risked glancing around. The room was crowded and smoky, but I didn't see too many of the self-righteous Bible-thumpers or derelicts I had expected. There were people of all ages, and most were African Americans. Some were well dressed, but I focused only on the relatively few obvious street people. The man finished reading, smiled, and said, "I'd especially like to welcome the newcomers here tonight." My heart sank and I thought, "Has it come to this?" Yes, it had. I had never thought I would find myself in a church basement with a bunch of drunks, but here I was. The chairperson asked if anyone new would like to introduce themselves, and I submerged even deeper below my collar, certain that no one would mistake me for a newcomer.

Then strange things began to happen. People raised their hands and told the most intimate stories about themselves, and others laughed. I was baffled. Why would anyone humiliate themselves that way? And why was everyone laughing? There was absolutely nothing amusing to me about facing a life without a civilized cock-tail before or a good wine with dinner. The prospect was just too dreary. I was sure I'd never smile—much less laugh—ever again.

At one point I glanced at the front wall. About ten hand-let-tered signs were randomly hung. It was bad enough (for my obsessive mind) that hardly any of them were straight, but these simplistic "slogans" made me want to gag: *One Day at a Time*; *Think*; and *Live and Let Live*. One of what looked like two oversize eye-test charts was labeled "The Twelve Suggested Steps"; the other was "The Twelve Traditions." I didn't know what they said, because I could see only the word "God" and some sappy euphemisms like "Higher Power" that didn't fool me a bit. I had finally cut through my denial enough to consider the possibility that alcohol could be at the core of my problems, but now there was a new barrier to the future: all that God stuff. I was much too sophisticated to believe in a Creator God, and I despaired of being able to fit into a group that I instinctively knew was my last, best—and only—hope.

I went home that night and called the woman I had asked to be my AA sponsor (my spiritual guide in the program) that very morning, obviously a major mistake in judgment. I was totally steamed and whined, "Why did you send me to that meeting? I have nothing in common with all those people!"

She paused, then responded, "You're right. You don't have anything in common with them. They know how to keep things simple; you don't. They know how to be grateful; you don't. They know how to stay sober; you don't. Keep going back." Then she hung up.

I'd had my first lesson in that rare species of honesty known as tough love.

2

STRANGERS
LOVED ME
BACK TO LIFE

I CALLED MY SPONSOR back that first night with another complaint: "And what about 'God this' and 'God that' and people pretending that you don't have to be a Christian by referring to the 'Higher Power'? I hate *anything* to do with religion."

"It will take a while, but you'll see that there's a difference between religion and spirituality," she patiently replied.

"But how will I know I'm getting the spirituality part of AA if it isn't religion?" I persisted.

"You'll stop seeing it as *part* of AA and realize that the whole program is spiritual."

"But where do I start?"

"At meetings *every* day. With Step One."

And so I learned another lesson: willingness to "act as if"—not to pretend but rather to *take the actions* as if I believed in them. I went to a meeting every day and gradually moved from the back of the room closer to the front. People began to learn my name, even if I couldn't remember theirs. I didn't know how they knew I was a newcomer until many years later when I saw a picture of me taken during those first months.

I didn't stop drinking right away. At some level I was still trying to prove to myself that I could control alcohol by having an occasional nightcap or glass of wine with dinner. With hindsight I can affirm that the AA program works much better if we don't drink . . . But I kept going back to meetings.

I never cease to be amazed at the seemingly small things that can help an alcoholic self-diagnose her or his disease. For me, it happened in two stages. As part of proving to myself that I really wasn't an alcoholic, I embarked on an experiment: According to one early writer about alcoholism, an alcoholic can't have a minimum of one and a maximum of three drinks a day, every day, for six weeks, without losing control. I had been a controlled drinker (in public) and a periodic drunk ("a scared daily drinker") for years and was confident that this exercise would prove that I wasn't an alcoholic—that I was just crazy. The first part of my awakening to life occurred on my thirty-fifth birthday.

This birthday was a biggie—one of the -5s and -0s that our culture makes into milestones. I wanted to celebrate in style, so I invited a few friends to my apartment for drinks, then we'd go to a fine French restaurant for dinner. At some point that day, I realized that I had planned my whole birthday celebration around those three drinks of my little experiment. I wanted to have cocktails at my place because I could have just one and it would be "big enough" (read "a water glass of scotch"). I chose a particular restaurant not because it had the best food but because it had the largest red-wine glasses. I was getting a sense of my own dance with denial, and the niggling question of whether a nonalcoholic would act that way began to gnaw at me.

I was reminded of that day some years later when the alcoholism authority Dr. LeClair Bissell described denial/rationaliza-tion to me in terms of broccoli: Imagine saying, "I only eat broccoli after 5 PM"; "I only eat *top-drawer* broccoli"; "I ate so much broccoli I threw up and then ate some more"; "How can I get married without broccoli?" and all the other absurd excuses we alcoholics come up with when we try to "control" our drinking.

Three weeks later I was walking through Central Park with a friend. It was one of those magical early autumn days when the sky is so clear you think you must have washed your eyeballs, and the turning leaves verge on gaudy. I had just a moment of being one with my world—a source of healing that had abandoned me three years earlier. During that time, I had always held out the possibility of suicide "if things got too bad," but in that split second I made a decision to live. That choice was completely incompatible with my denial around my own alcoholism. My whole life didn't pass before my eyes, but a lot of it did, especially the worst parts, and I knew I had to stop drinking to hold to my resolve to live. In that moment of clarity I saw that every time I drank, horrible things *didn't* happen to me, but every time disaster had struck—violent arguments, rape, job problems, relationship breakups, suicide attempts—I had been drinking. I had had my last drink.

When I went to St. Luke's that night, I hesitatingly raised my hand for the first time and whispered that I am an alcoholic. People cheered and clapped and cried and hugged me and told me they'd been praying for me. If their response surprised me, my own astonished me: I burst into tears of relief. For the next year every time I went to a meeting I sat down and started crying. I eventually figured out that an AA meeting was the only place I felt safe, though I didn't know from what. The people around me would put their arms around me and hold me. In those early days I was filled with grief and shame and feelings of being unlovable, and those strangers I thought were so different from me loved me back to life until I joined the human race and could begin to love myself.

There was a meeting focused on the Twelve Steps at St. Luke's on Friday night, so I jumped into the steps with all the compulsiveness with which I had drunk.

3

ONE STEP
AT A TIME

I WAS SO IMPATIENT to "get it" that "One Day at a Time" to me meant surmounting twelve steps in twelve days. I slowly and thoughtfully read through the Twelve Steps (see Appendix) and was confident that I had mastered them after that one, careful reading. Just to make certain, I bought the AA book *Twelve Steps and Twelve Traditions* and read it. Then I wasn't too sure. Soon I discovered that almost all the step meetings in New York City start with Step One the first week of a new year so that most of the meetings are on the same step the same week. So it is possible for the truly possessed to go to a meeting on the same step every night of the week. I did. But the closer I came to the end of each week, the less convinced I was that I'd really gotten that week's step. In fact, nearly every day since I first thought this, I've had an *a-ha!* experience about what physical, mental, and emotional recovery is about, and I've come to the conclusion that I don't have the wisdom or imagination to ever completely "get it." For that, I am grateful. I never get bored.

The Twelve Steps have given me a roadmap for living through the transformations of recovery. Whenever I have had a problem, I've known that the answer lay in one of the steps. Unfortunately, in early sobriety, more often than not I picked the wrong step to try to solve my problem of the moment—I frequently tried to make amends, for example, when I should have been "turning it over." And in each step, I slammed into at least one word that stopped me cold or that I somehow didn't see at all. I nevertheless embraced the steps "as if" I trusted every word, and I began to heal. Anyway.

Initially, what cracked my resistance to the steps was the fact that they were written in the past tense. They were not commandments—not even that evasive Higher Power was telling me what to do—but rather were descriptions of how the first hundred members of AA got and stayed sober. To describe the fullness of my spiritual journey in Alcoholics Anonymous and Buddhism, I must begin by sharing briefly my experiences in working with the steps, for today they are inseparable for me from the Dharma, the Buddha's teachings.

STEP ONE: WE ADMITTED WE WERE POWERLESS OVER ALCOHOL—THAT OUR LIVES HAD BECOME UNMANAGEABLE.

In the first step, I encountered not one but *three* words that tripped me up: *we, powerless,* and *unmanageable*. I had never been a *we*. I had always been an *I*. I didn't even like *wes*; they were *weak*. I was captain of my ship and had always believed that I would go down with it if it sank because no one, ever, would really help me. My sponsor kept throwing one of those detestable slogans at me: *Identify—Don't Compare* (with other alcoholics). I had to overcome my terminal uniqueness to even begin to see the way alcoholism had affected my life.

The more meetings I went to, the more I heard my own story from the lips of others who were painfully honest about themselves. I began to see that I truly was the same as these people when it came to my relationship with alcohol. Decades earlier the American Medical Association had labeled alcoholism a disease, and the so-called medical model was very helpful to my acceptance that I was not weak or immoral any more than someone who has a heart attack is. I pacified myself with physical analogies: if human beings weren't the same physically, there could never be any such thing as a heart Pacemaker or even an aspirin that would be helpful to everyone with a weak heart or headache—it only makes sense that if alcoholism is a disease I'd have the same symptoms and experience the same progression as others with the same disease. I got a handle on *we*, if only in relationship to alcoholism.

During my childhood in Texas, I was taught that I was not powerless over anything. If I had enough grit and worked hard enough, I could have power over anything. I grew up into an incomparable Control Queen. I had a hard time seeing my powerlessness over alcohol because of my ability to control—up to a point—my drinking. I drank with people who drank like me, or worse than I did, and I had a serious case of *Yet*—focusing on all the bad things that had never happened to me . . . yet.

One day when I was several years sober, I was describing the tell-tale signs of alcoholism to a friend, and I began to talk about blackouts—those occasions when you've drunk so much that you walk and talk and appear normal but later can't remember a period of time, perhaps only a few minutes but sometimes hours. Blackouts are almost always a sure sign of alcoholism, at least for any drinker who wasn't scared silly enough by the first one to not let it happen again. I recalled situations where I could remember sitting down at a dinner party but not getting up or, more ominously, getting on a New York City subway train late at night but not getting off. I blushed with shame over those hell holes of amnesia concerning what I had done or said or where I had parked the car (and looking to see if there were any dents or blood). I dreaded being introduced to someone who said, "You probably don't remember me but . . . " and wondering if in a drunken stupor I had slept with him. With a jolt I realized that nothing could be more powerless than being in a blackout.

I began to realize that when I took the first drink I could not predict what would happen if I took another, and I always did take another. Having admitted that on occasion I had been powerless over alcohol, I began to find more and more things that I was powerless over—perhaps everything except my own attitudes. I knew

I had no real control over the weather, for example, but for most of my life I had not accepted that I couldn't control the emotional storms of my life partner. It finally dawned on me that *my* emotional comfort depended on how I *related* to life's daily challenges, not to the people or events in my world.

But was my life *unmanageable*? No way. I was the youngest *this* and the only woman *that* and was well respected throughout my profession. Look at how much money I had earned! My tough-love sponsor disabused me of those inflated notions quickly. She asked if I thought someone whose life was manageable would attempt suicide, three times no less, and how much money I was bringing in *now*, living in one room on disability insurance, unable to work at all. I got it—but again only in relationship to alcohol.

STEP TWO: CAME TO BELIEVE THAT A POWER GREATER THAN OURSELVES COULD RESTORE US TO SANITY.

This was the first step where I had to deal with "a Power greater than ourselves." Though unwritten, *God* was the word I had to accommodate. At first I went with a fairly common sequence of reading and understanding the step: *Came . . .* , then *Came to . . .* , then *Came to believe . . . .* I had indeed come. I was coming to, and I was coming to believe, in the sense of "coming *in order* to believe." What I was believing is that if all the people I heard sharing their lives at meetings could make it, perhaps I could too. I was beginning to have the tiniest flickers of spiritual fire: I was beginning to feel hope.

I heard a number of people grappling with the idea of a Higher Power and *G-O-D* as an acronym for *Good Orderly Direction*, for example. I decided on *Group of Drunks*. The consensus was that everyone needs to recognize a greater Power and to realize that they aren't it. I was comfortable using the people at the AA meetings as the power that could restore me to sanity. On the question of sanity, when I first came to AA I didn't think I was an alcoholic but was convinced that I was crazy—as proved by my stays in psychiatric hospitals. When I latched on to the concept of alcoholism as a disease, I decided that I might be sick but I didn't believe I was crazy. Then one day I heard myself say, "I'd be crazy to drink again," and I realized that I *had* been insane when I was drinking and would be again if I picked up.

People with some years of comfortable sobriety suggested very strongly that newcomers not only have a Higher Power but also *pray* to Her/Him/It/Them. Time to "act as if" again. One of my favorite recordings was the Beatles's *White Album*, so I took the *HP* from *Higher Power* and paid homage to one of their tunes: Honey Pie. I envisioned Honey Pie as a fluffy, warm, older woman, not at all the kind of figure who would give me whiplash every time I thought of God. I prayed (talked a lot) to Honey Pie and discovered that prayer works. I'm not quite sure how—whether Someone was really listening, whether my willingness to act as if carried me along, or whether I just couldn't think more than one thought at a time and so if I was praying I wasn't obsessing about who did or might do me wrong. (I was to learn that this kind of focused invocation was working for me the same way that meditation would later—see Chapter 9.) Honey Pie worked so well for me that I began lending her to others going through the same agnostic struggle, and soon there was an enthusiastic coterie singing the praises of HP. What we all shared was that our prayers were expressions of gratitude.

STEP THREE: MADE A DECISION TO TURN OUR WILL AND OUR LIVES OVER TO THE CARE OF GOD *as we understood [god]*.

For a long time, I simply didn't see the words *made a decision* and *to the care of* and thought I had to turn my will and my life over to God. When I finally realized that it was to the *care of* my Group of Drunks that I was turning my will and my life over, it was easy for me to *make the decision* to do so. In fact, I had made that decision the first time I had admitted my alcoholism and asked for help.

As long as I had tried to take care of everything in my life alone, I had failed miserably. But the members of my "home group," at St. Luke's, wanted only the best for me: sobriety. I could risk trusting their experience, strength, and hope because it would always lead me away from a drink, not toward one.

Eventually, I even overcame another misreading—that of turning various people and situations over to God. It always came back to my working on myself, because I began to see I was powerless over others.

STEP FOUR: MADE A SEARCHING AND FEARLESS MORAL INVENTORY OF OURSELVES.

The idea of a moral inventory seemed at first contradictory if I had a disease. But I was painfully aware that I was still feeling shame and guilt about the past, when many of my actions clearly had *not* been moral—especially in the time I "stole" from employers and the affection I stole from people married to someone besides me—and I had to deal with them to resolve those feelings. At first the notion of a fearless inventory seemed absurd, until I realized that although learning more about my deep dark secrets might not be very pleasant, it was what I did not know that I had to fear. Inventories tell us what's on the shelf, and whether we have too little or too much—this was what I needed to identify to become a whole, happy person, which by this step had gone beyond being a possibility to becoming a goal.

In my compulsive way, I used the books *Alcoholics Anonymous* and *Twelve Steps and Twelve Traditions*, several Step Four guidebooks, every old address book I could find, and a lot of yellow pads. Ever the perfectionist, I wasn't about to miss anything or anybody. I followed the advice to write out my inventory, which was a most wise decision. I was able to read through the final inventory and circle a wide variety of behaviors, most of which were expressions fear, that seemed to fall repeatedly into the same few patterns. This way I was able to bring the patterns into the present moment rather than just staring at individual incidents in the past.

I had written a fourth step with no intention of doing the fifth, but I was so emotionally peeled by the process that I called my sponsor immediately and asked if we could get together.

STEP FIVE: ADMITTED TO GOD, TO OURSELVES, AND TO ANOTHER HUMAN BEING THE EXACT NATURE OF OUR WRONGS.

Until I sat down with my sponsor to "do" Step Five, I had not focused on the words *exact nature*. As I talked with her, I found that by myself, I was incapable of getting to the exact nature. I repeatedly exaggerated, in one direction or another—I minimized the negative and maximized the positive some times and did just the opposite at others. At one minute I said, "I never hurt anyone except myself," but the next insisted, "I've hurt every person I've ever been close to." Neither statement was true, but I couldn't see that by myself. As we went through my inventory, to the best of my ability I admitted the exact nature of my wrongs to myself and another human being.

As I began to see my patterns more clearly I realized that I was increasingly sharing them with the Group of Drunks at my home meeting. And I began to change. A major discovery for me in doing Step Four, to give but one example, was how very difficult it is for me to let people give to me. When I talked about this in meetings, other people spoke up about how this limitation affects them and what they try to do about it. Somehow by just talking aloud about it—admitting the exact nature to a Group of

Drunks—about 90 percent of that behavior evaporated. My AA friends were all too willing to take up my invitation to call me on it for the other 10 percent of the time. I began to grow, but even more important, I began to trust.

Trusting anyone had always been very difficult for me. But I acted as if and trusted one person—my sponsor—with everything I thought was wrong with me. Mostly her response was nodding understanding or even laughter at my lack of originality. I slowly enlarged the circle within my home group, trusting them with those awful secrets, and gradually opening to more and more people. Today I have no secrets, from anyone, and that's amazingly freeing.

STEP SIX: WERE ENTIRELY READY TO HAVE GOD REMOVE ALL THESE DEFECTS OF CHARACTER.

When I reached Step Six, all the step meetings in New York City couldn't get me through or past it. Looking back, I realize that the biggest problem was that I did not see the word *ready* but through some kind of mental alchemy had put *willing* in its place. Actually, the conversion wasn't totally mysterious: *Twelve Steps and Twelve Traditions* talks extensively about willingness for this step, and I simply forgot that that wasn't what Step Six itself said.

From my first day of sobriety and through no virtue or merit of my own, I was graced with willingness—to go to meetings, to call my sponsor, to act *as if* when I needed to. I really was willing to let go of my "defects of character," but I was in no way *ready*. These failings were nothing less than my barrier of defenses against the world that I had vigilantly erected during my thirty-five years. I could not let go of them until I could put something else in their place. I believed, for example, that I really needed my anger—it was righteous and constructive because it spurred me to social activism against the injustices of the world.

In the belief often expressed at AA meetings that alcoholism is a threefold disease—physical, mental, and spiritual—I decided to try to become ready to let go of destructive characteristics like anger on all three fronts. Physically, I paid close attention to my diet and began to do strenuous exercise daily, and because our minds and bodies are inseparable, I grew stronger, more confident, calmer. I addressed the mental front by beginning to see a therapist. Step Four addresses the *whats* rather than the *whys* of behavior, so I used that inventory as the basis for unearthing the foundations of my most deeply lodged defenses. Spiritually, I went to as many meetings as I could to learn from my sober brothers and sisters about gratitude and hope and faith and joy and laughter. These great gifts of the spirit began to displace the negativity, fear, and anger that had been barely below the surface. Just how the negative energies worked in me became clear when I turned to the seventh step.

STEP SEVEN: HUMBLY ASKED [THE HIGHER POWER] TO REMOVE OUR SHORTCOMINGS.

I took a long time to get past the first word of this step: *Humbly.* I deeply believed that *humility* and *humiliation* were interchangeable concepts, and I'd suffered too much of the latter while I was drinking to voluntarily revisit that condition in sobriety.

One night a man at a seventh step meeting defined *humility* as "an accurate assessment of our assets and liabilities." That definition captured both the spirit and the letter of my shortcomings, as I had discovered when I was trying to determine the "exact nature of my wrongs" when I took Step Four.

This awakening took me back to the seventh step chapter in *Twelve Steps and Twelve Traditions*, when I truly read for the first time—though it had been there all the while—this statement: "The chief activator of our defects has been self-centered fear— primarily fear that we would lose something we already possessed or would fail to get something we demanded." A few years later, this same sentence would open my mind to several key Dharma issues about the relationship of self, attachment, and suffering, but for now it elicited my frequent response to new ideas: I tried to argue with them. Perhaps some defects, but surely not all.

My search for a "fear-free defect" led to one of those unasked-for growth opportunities that so resemble peeling an onion, complete with tears. I had looked back over the recent years of depression, with the help of my therapist, to discover that sure enough, all that depression was masking in-turned anger. At this point I had both depression *and* anger, and when I tried to stop smoking I was dubbed The Towering Inferno. But when I painfully flayed another layer of denial, I discovered that self-centered fear was indeed fueling the anger—fear of loss, of abandonment, of not getting what I needed, of losing what I had. And the more deeply I peeled, the more my certainty increased that self-centered fear underlay everything that consistently made me uncomfortable ("things that consistently make me uncomfortable" was and is my working definition of *shortcomings, character defects, wrongs*, and the like).

In some distress over what to do about the fear, I began to heed two more of those odious slogans everyone was tossing around: *Live in the Now* and *This Too Shall Pass*. (I would later see that these slogans express two key tenets of Buddhism: reality exists only in this moment, and impermanence.)

Given to frequent lapses into the horrible past or projecting into the threatening future, I was the target of these lovingly hurled clichés more often than most of the others. Even as I raised my mental shield against them, I had the insight that the only times I felt fear—or its cousins anxiety, nervousness, worry, or apprehension—were when I was not living in the moment. I was not capable of being simultaneously afraid and in the now. If I was willing to give up my scary stories and come back into the present, I found that I could do so quite quickly either by focusing intently on a physical action or by concentrating on a word or phrase, which a few years later I would learn are two of the four foundations of mindfulness meditation practice.

STEP EIGHT: MADE A LIST OF ALL PERSONS WE HAD HARMED, AND BECAME WILLING TO MAKE AMENDS TO THEM ALL.

This step looked like a cakewalk. All I had to do was make a list of persons I had harmed—they were all there in my written fourth step, I thought—and be willing to make amends to them, which

I felt I was. The crucial word in this step was *them*, all those other people I had harmed.

I was all set to move on to Step Nine when I heard a woman whose story I identified with a lot talk about the eighth step. I was digesting what she said about putting her own name at the top of the list when she stunned me by adding that she next had to put down the names of all the people who had harmed her, because she had been a *compliant victim*. Suddenly I saw how many times I had been "victimized" because I had put myself in the position to be, out of self-centered fear, and how much mileage I had gotten out of pity—especially self-pity—for all the "terrible things" that had been done to me.

As agonizing as it was for me to look again at all the ways I knew I had harmed myself through drinking, I now had to look at my role in all the painful interactions that I had been blaming on others. I found that I consistently had set myself up for suffering by making other people my Higher Power. It worked well for me to do this in AA, with people in my Group of Drunks who wanted only the best for me. But when I was drinking, I gave power and control to people who were doing the same dance with self-centered fear that I was doing, and the results were repeatedly the same: I felt unloved and unlovable, abandoned and rejected, victimized. It took me much self-examination to realize that it takes, as they say, two to tango, and I had relentlessly chosen to give power to people who would confirm my worst beliefs about myself.

STEP NINE: MADE DIRECT AMENDS TO SUCH PEOPLE WHEREVER POSSIBLE, EXCEPT WHEN TO DO SO WOULD INJURE THEM OR OTHERS.

The challenge for me was to make *direct* amends to people I had harmed, and it took me many years to find an authentic way to make amends to those who had harmed me. Many of these people had been out of my life for so long that I had no idea how to find them. Even if I could find them, the potential for causing pain and "injury" to myself or others was great in such circumstances as involving someone whose marriage I had broken up or a partner I had been unfaithful to. Other "wrongdoings"—especially to my parents—were "sins of omission." I simply wasn't present for them.

Because *amend* literally means "to make right, to improve" and I had put my name at the top of the Step Eight list, I clearly had to start with myself, first, by staying sober and, second, by developing the awareness I needed not to hurt others or force them into positions to hurt me. Above all, I had to forgive myself. For those people I could not find, I looked for some way—perhaps by volunteer work or a donation—that might in some way compensate by helping someone else. For friends and family I had basically ignored for years, I looked for opportunities to tell them I was truly sorry for my absences, in some cases talking about my alcoholism but not in others, depending on what "harm" that information might do. I mentally made a commitment to be present for the people I loved and who loved me, in person when I could or by email or note when I could not.

As my sponsor suggested, I tried praying for people who had harmed me, but this did not work terribly well for me. I found myself telling Honey Pie I wished dreadful misfortunes would befall those people who had harmed me. It was not until some years later when I learned the practice of *metta* ("lovingkindness") meditation that I could with an open heart understand how their own pain had caused their actions toward me and sincerely wish them well (see Chapter 14).

STEP TEN: CONTINUED TO TAKE PERSONAL INVENTORY, AND WHEN WE WERE WRONG PROMPTLY ADMITTED IT.

Doing the fourth and fifth steps had been so rewarding for me that I had no problem continuing to take inventory. Many of my AA friends made a list at the end of each *day* of their problems—but that kind of review was not practical for an insomniac like me. I would have been awake all night fretting about how to make amends and how promptly I could do so. Instead, whenever I found myself uncomfortable about something, I stopped what I was doing, drew myself into the present moment, and tried to figure out what was going on. (My instant time-out room at work was often a bathroom stall.) If amends needed to be made, I sometimes made them immediately. Other times, I called my sponsor first and did a Step 5½ to double-check that I really was in touch with the *exact* nature of my wrong.

For most of my life I simply was not spontaneous because I was unwilling to risk making a mistake. I thought I had to justify my existence by being perfect. When I began to work the tenth step, I was amazed by the sense of relief that came when I apologized for being wrong. And I never alienated a single friend by admitting a mistake as long as I was taking my own inventory and not theirs.

STEP ELEVEN: SOUGHT THROUGH PRAYER AND MEDITATION TO IMPROVE OUR CONSCIOUS CONTACT WITH GOD *as we understood [god],* PRAYING ONLY FOR KNOWLEDGE OF [GOD'S] WILL FOR US AND THE POWER TO CARRY THAT OUT.

Since I had already come up with "Group of Drunks" for the word *God*, this was the first step where nothing derailed me before I even started. I strongly adhered to the characterization of *prayer* as talking and *meditation* as listening. These definitions worked perfectly for me in AA meetings. When I raised my hand to share a problem, I was asking for help, whether I knew it or not. When others responded, Honey Pie clearly spoke through them. HP's will for me, always, was to stay sober, and others' sharing gave me the strength I needed to do so.

I was quite comfortable with this working of Step Eleven for many years, but eventually I realized that something was missing. I had always been a spiritual seeker, so I began again the quest for something unknown but holy. Part Two of this book is about that search.

STEP TWELVE: HAVING HAD A SPIRITUAL AWAKENING AS THE RESULT OF THESE STEPS, WE TRIED TO CARRY THIS MESSAGE TO ALCOHOLICS, AND TO PRACTICE THESE PRINCIPLES IN ALL OUR AFFAIRS.

My misreading of this step was not recognizing that the spiritual awakening happens "as the result of these steps." In a sense I was working—or at least trying to work—all the steps from my first meeting, and I benefited from being consciously aware of them from the beginning. But the steps are in order for a reason, and an old-timer gave me the excellent advice that if I was having trouble with a step, I should go back to the one before it, and maybe to the one before that one. I wake up physically slowly, and my spiritual awakening has also been "patient" and the result of assimilating the steps into my life seemingly at a cellular level.

The reason my sponsor sent me to St. Luke's in the first place, she later told me, was because that group has a strong emphasis on service—on carrying the message to alcoholics—and learning to live the steps in everyday life. I learned that "service" could mean many things—just being at a meeting is a way of "witnessing" that this program works. She gave me no choice but to do service from day one: The first week, I began making coffee for the St. Luke's meeting. Later my sponsor encouraged me to stay involved by saying that I could eventually also do service by greeting newcomers at meetings, answering hotline telephones, sponsoring people, speaking at meetings, holding office, volunteering to do institutional work at hospitals and prisons—the list is as long as one's imagination. When we comprehend the devastation that alcoholism causes in our lives and others', most of us are deeply moved to try to give something back, in gratitude for what we have been given in recovery.

I was so grateful for the transformation in my own life—I went from being a severe depressive to a woman nicknamed Doris Day and Pollyanna by my friends—that I enthusiastically volunteered for many kinds of service, and I credit my continuous sobriety and happiness to my ongoing service assignments. No service affected me more profoundly than taking AA meetings into maximum-security women's prisons for about six years.

When I went into a prison meeting to tell my story for the first time, I was greeted by hostile stares that probably looked much like the ones I gave the people around me at my first meeting. "Who is this whitey do-gooder?" they seemed to say. I just told my story—what it had been like, how I got to AA, what it was like now. It was fairly early in my sobriety, and I was very close to my pain. My voice thickened and tears filled my eyes as I talked about my despair and hopelessness and inability to even imagine that anything could ever change. When I looked around, I saw the tears of identification in several women's eyes, and many came up to me and said, "Please keep coming back." I did.

All but two of the inmates at my first prison meeting were women of color, most involved in a drug- and alcohol-rehabilitation program. Some spoke no English but came to the meeting anyway, perhaps for the coffee or to impress counselors but often for the fellowship of others like themselves. Many women were serving mandatory five-year sentences for selling controlled substances, but a few had life sentences for violent crimes, including killing their own children while in blackouts. The illiteracy rate was quite high—we sometimes had trouble finding women who could read well enough to read the Preamble and Twelve Steps at the beginning of the meeting. But most of the women in this program were going to school—some to learn to read and write, others to get their high school equivalency degrees, a few taking video distance-learning courses for college credits.

I soon learned that I am no different from these women. Only an accident of birth landed me in fancy psychiatric hospitals while they ended up in prison. But we have the same disease. We are alcoholics. My empathic compassion for and identification with them planted the seeds in my heart for the interconnectedness with all beings that would flower through Buddhism.

4

PROMISES OF
THINGS TO COME

WHEN I WAS IN early sobriety, one of the most offensive remarks anyone made to me was "May you be blessed with a slow recovery." I had always been a fast study, and I wanted to know everything and to be "ready for graduation" immediately. Fortunately for me, the blessings of recovery were indeed bestowed upon me gradually. If I had known or thought or felt any part of the kaleidoscopic process one day earlier than I did, I truly believe I could not have handled any of it. I couldn't recover any faster than I did. I couldn't be healthy any faster than I was.

One of my AA friends maintains that "first it [life, recovery] gets better, then it gets worse, then it gets different, then it gets real." About the time that I entered the "gets different" stage, I began to go to an AA topic meeting that focuses on certain promises—among many—found in the book *Alcoholics Anonymous*:

- We are going to know a new freedom and a new happiness.
- We will not regret the past nor wish to shut the door on it.
- We will comprehend the word *serenity* and we will know peace.
- No matter how far down the scale we have gone, we will see how our experience can benefit others.
- That feeling of uselessness and self-pity will disappear.
- We will lose interest in selfish things and gain interest in our fellows.
- Self-seeking will slip away.
- Our whole attitude and outlook upon life will change.
- Fear of people and of economic insecurity will leave us.
- We will intuitively know how to handle situations that used to baffle us.
- We will suddenly realize that God is doing for us what we could not do for ourselves. (4th edition, pp. 83–84)

Much to my amazement, and overflowing gratitude, these promises were coming true in my life—and my life was indeed different, but it would not become entirely "real" for a few more years. I can mark my progress/process on the spiritual journey of recovery during this time by highlighting a few of these particular promises.

We are going to know a new freedom and a new happiness.

The connotation of *freedom* changed for me from freedom *to* to freedom *from*. More than anything else, I was free from the control of addiction. Only with hindsight was I able to see how I had unconsciously structured much of my life around drinking and drinking situations. As long as I was thinking about the next drink—when, where, whether I needed to worry about driving—I was not a free person. It was as if I was a marionette controlled by a psychotic puppeteer: myself.

At first, I wasn't quite sure what to do with my newfound freedom, but I soon began to explore who this new person was and what she liked. I began to do things that I would have never dreamed of doing during my drinking career—unless I had happened to be very drunk at the moment. My first excursion into new territory was to take up belly dancing, which I loved and did as a preferred kind of exercise until my aging hip joints started to complain too much.

My next big adventure—the result of teasing a committed motorcyclist during a fuel shortage—was to take up riding motorcycles, which I had not even thought of doing until the day I decided I wanted to, fortunately after I got sober. Over a period of twenty-five years I had five bikes: Freedom I (Honda 500), Freedom II (Honda 950), Freedom III (Shadow 750), Freedom IV (Shadow 1100), and Freedom V (Magna 750). At least once a year I would "run away from home": I'd get on my bike with a mountain tent and camping gear strapped to the back and take off for wherever my nose seemed to be pointed that day. I might end up on the Skyline Drive in Virginia or perhaps on Cape Breton in Nova Scotia. The one constant was that I sought out AA meetings whenever I camped near a town that had one. Because I had the slogan *Easy Does It* on my helmet, I met other sober bikers along the way, including one motorcycle club known as Chapter 5 (the chapter with the Twelve Steps in the book *Alcoholics Anonymous*) and another called the Sober Angels. I only stopped riding when health problems made it no longer safe for me, and I felt that my freedom had been literally curtailed.

At first, happiness was simply feeling better physically. I could recall all those mornings when I had said, "I would be so happy if I just didn't have this hangover." And to that I added, "this shame, this embarrassment, this fear, this guilt." Well into sobriety, I decided that happiness amounts to wanting what you have. Earlier, I might have wanted what I had, but I was never satisfied with how much of it there was. I always wanted more. When I got sober and people told me I had to pray, I usually carried on a running monolog directed at Honey Pie. I "acted as if" and said thank you for everything I had that I really didn't need, whether I felt gratitude or not. Some of my soliloquies went like this: "Honey Pie, I'm glad the stoplight is red so that truck won't hit me." "Honey Pie, I'm glad the light is green so I can cross the street." "Honey Pie, I'm grateful that I have a pillow and sheets on my bed, a bed, pictures on the wall, a hot shower, a radio, good food, a dog." And always "I'm grateful for sobriety." Somewhere along the way, I began to change, and I became truly grateful for all the blessings in my life. With gratitude, I could happily want what I had. It was enough.

We will not regret the past nor wish to shut the door on it.

Regrets for the past stayed with me for quite a long time, along with shame, grief, and anger. Working with my sponsor on the fourth and fifth steps helped me let go of many of the regrets. The disease concept of alcoholism did much to dispel most of my guilt about my actions and sometimes my lack of actions during active alcoholism.

The regret I had the most trouble letting go of was my rage at the doctors who had left me memory-impaired from shock treatments because they didn't know enough about alcoholism to recognize it. The first time this constriction loosened at all for me was a time fairly early in sobriety when a group of us went out for coffee after an AA meeting. Conversation turned to the *Wizard of Oz*, and people were comparing themselves to various characters: "I'm the one who had no heart," "I'm the one who had no brain," etc. I burst into tears because although I had read about a book a day since I was a teen, I couldn't remember any of them, including the *Wizard of Oz*. One of the women gently said to me, "Even if you can't remember any of those books, they changed you in ways that no one can ever take away."

A few years later a man at an AA meeting said, "Everything in my life had to happen for me to be here, and for that I am grateful." I suddenly realized that the same thing was true for me, including the shock treatments. My brain had always been my primary defense system between me and the world, and if it hadn't been rendered—at least temporarily—nonfunctional, I could have never gotten sober. I had to have a "broken brain" to be teachable.

We will comprehend the word *serenity* and we will know peace.

Before I got sober, I don't think I ever experienced serenity. I was always worried about something, usually my ability to control that something. But I knew that serenity was possible out there in the future, because almost every AA meeting had a poster with the adapted version of Reinhold Niebuhr's Serenity Prayer, which is widely used to open or close meetings:

THE SERENITY PRAYER

God,
Grant me the serenity to accept the things
   I cannot change,
The courage to change the things I can,
And the wisdom to know the difference.

It took me quite a while to memorize this prayer, but it became the foundation for my ability to cope with the distresses of everyday life, small and large. When my mind cleared enough for me to contemplate it, I saw it as a beautifully articulated summary of the Twelve Steps, which took me much longer to learn. "The serenity to accept the things I cannot change" for me refers to the first, second, and third steps: admitting to powerlessness, coming to believe that a power other than me could restore me to sanity, and making a decision to turn my will and life over to its care, sometimes expressed at meetings as "I can't. God can. I think I'll let God do it."

I found the parallel for "the courage to change the things I can" in Steps Four through Ten: doing a searching inventory, admitting the exact nature of wrongs, being ready to let go of them and asking for help in doing so, listing people harmed and making amends to them, and continuing to take inventory and admitting when we are wrong. For me, "the wisdom to know the difference" lay in the eleventh and twelfth steps: seeking through prayer and meditation the knowledge of wise action, drawing in the strength to take wise action at AA meetings and to help other alcoholics as we practice the steps in everyday life.

Whenever I have remembered to be mindful about integrating the Serenity Prayer into my life, I have truly known peace as well as serenity.

Self-seeking will slip away.

A great deal of my self-seeking was related to my "I am what I do" identity. In AA, no one knew my occupation, or cared. No one knew my last name, or cared. There was no way to earn a higher degree or a black belt or a gold medal. Even holding office in an AA group is considered doing service rather than being recognized as an honor, and officers rotate out before they can become too fond of their "status." When we've made the decision to try to have humility, in the sense of accurate self-perception, it is inevitable that we turn away from our own navel and work the twelfth step, doing service to help other alcoholics.

Also, as I noted in the Preface, anonymity is the foundation of spiritual growth. For this reason, remaining anonymous at the public level greatly enhances our ability to let go of self-seeking.

Fear of people and of economic insecurity will leave us.

We will intuitively know how to handle situations that used to baffle us.

I was never asked to believe anything about Alcoholics Anonymous on blind faith. Ample evidence for everything positive I hope for surrounds me at every AA meeting. Over time, after repeatedly hearing people in meetings describe the loss of a loved one, or a job, or a dream but staying sober and turning a difficult incident into an opportunity for spiritual growth, most of us begin to gain hope that perhaps we can ride out our bad patches too and arrive at a better place. With more time, the hope turns to confidence. We begin to develop faith—in ourselves, in others, in the workings of our Higher Power.

With faith, we increasingly trust those who have traveled on this journey with us. Another very old AA slogan is *We are as sick as we are secret*, sometimes phrased *We are as sick as our secrets*. We soon find that others have no secrets from us and eventually we too have no secrets. We have nothing to fear because of the repeated confirmation that when we are in the present, no one knows anything about us that can hurt us. The circle of the promised blessings is complete, and we know a new freedom.

My faith was to be profoundly tested after I had about two decades of recovery in AA. Everything in my life seemed ideal and all the blessings promised on pages 83 and 84 of the Big Book had come true for me. But in the short space of several years, I lost everything that I thought mattered to me except sobriety. My health, my career, and a long-term committed relationship evaporated, and suddenly none of those promises *seemed* to be authentically in my life. But in reality the blessings never left me. All those anonymous friends who had loved me back to life years earlier were still here for me, along with new friends in and out of AA. Most of all, through working Step Eleven, I now had a spiritual underpinning that was like steel reinforcement for the Twelve Steps I feared might yet crumble beneath my feet. I looked at the promise that "No matter how far down the scale we have gone, we will see how our experience can benefit others," and began the search to share my experiences that has resulted in this book.

Part Two:

Buddha

"I am a Buddhist."

5

LOOKING FOR
THE BUDDHA

"DO YOU MEAN there is not a word in Nepali for *thank you?*"
I asked. It was the second day of my trip to the Himalayas. Whenever I've traveled, I've tried to learn a few basic words in the host
language—terms like *please, thank you, where, latrine, how long,
how much.* I felt exasperated because I had not been able to find
thank you in any guide or phrase book.

The Sherpa, one of our guides for the year-end trek into the
Gorkha Himal, spoke excellent English. He smiled at the question
he had heard from other baffled Westerners and replied, "There is

no word. Why would you want to thank someone for doing what they're meant to be doing?"

As we walked through the cobbled streets of Kathmandu to the bus that would take us out of the valley, I'm not sure whether my mouth or my eyes gaped more widely. I had been in so-called developing countries before, but nothing had prepared me for the poverty and harsh life of many Nepali people in 1984. I literally had no frame of reference for what I encountered—everything was new to me.

The six-hour bus trip to our trailhead was bouncy and harrowing. The only law of the road seemed to be to blow the horn when rounding a curve on the unpaved, single-lane road with a 3,000-foot drop-off on one side, below which were strewn carcasses of trucks and buses that hadn't quite made it. The farther we went from Kathmandu, the farther back in time we wound. After our second night's camp, two days' walk beyond where the bus could go, we were back in the Stone Age: I saw no metal tools. The plows and digging tools were made of wood or horn. Mountainsides were terraced within an inch of their lives, with unrecognizable (to me) crops planted on every flat surface, no matter how small. Women bent and squatted to work the soil, which was so poor that at one end of a small field they were planting crops and at the other were cutting out from the same soil mud bricks to dry in the sun for buildings.

Whenever we stopped to rest, eat, or camp, children seemed to appear from nowhere with palms pressed together and were urgently piping, "*Namaste. Namaste.*" I returned their greetings, and they giggled and shrilly chanted even louder. I asked the Sherpa what exactly *namaste* means, and he replied, "The divine in me salutes the divine in you. So even if you're a criminal, what's holy in me can greet what's holy in you."

Nepal is a Hindu kingdom, so greetings from the divine in one person to the divine in another seemed quite logical to me. As we went higher in the Himalayas, we passed through the lands of several ethnic groups, readily distinguishable by their clothing, jewelry, and house construction. One day we saw prayer flags, and I knew from my reading that we were high enough to be moving now among Buddhist people. I was looking forward to reaching the first *gompa* (temple) and seeing "Buddhism in action" in its natural setting. We never saw a *gompa*—many of the villages had only five or seven houses—but what I was encountering nevertheless was the real living out of Buddhist teachings.

Here there clearly was no need for a word for *thank you*. Life and work were purposeful whatever one was doing—and people accepted that they were doing what they were supposed to be doing. "Real Buddhists" here didn't sit around reading scripture or chanting or collapsed into a pretzel contortion for meditating. They dug in the fields. They wove cloth. They carried firewood. They lived, simply, accepting the moment with purpose and were peaceful in a way that gave the word *serenity* a new meaning for me. They lived kindness and compassion. In a small village near the snow line I finally "got it"—that Buddhism is not a religion in the Western sense but rather is a way of living committed to not harming others, oneself, or one's world. With all the advantages and privileges of being born where and when I was, I found nevertheless that a quality of living that had eluded me all my life was rooted in a poor settlement in the Himalayas. I wanted what these people had, even though I didn't fully understand what it was or where to find it.

From AA's beginning, members have urged newcomers to try to go back to their religious roots and enhance their AA program with spiritual practice. I had gone back to my family's church and a number of my friends', but there just was not a good fit for me anywhere. I had been interested in Buddhism as a teenager, and now I saw the possibility of its being the path I sought.

When I returned home, I did what I always did when I wanted to learn about something: I read every book I could get my hands on. I didn't really understand much of what I encountered, but I kept on reading. I knew that meditation was part of this practice and I tackled that aspect of it with a vengeance. I read. I listened to tapes. I tried—knowing that meditation was good for me, my blood pressure, tension, insomnia. I sat miserably contorted, my mind racing madly from one complaint to another.

A friend who was quite amused by my latching on to yet another obsessive quest invited me to go to a Buddhist workshop called "How to Change the World." The teacher was the Vietnamese Zen monk Thich Nhat Hanh, whom Martin Luther King, Jr., had nominated for the Nobel Peace Prize for his antiwar activism. I eagerly accepted, imagining that I would go to a hall filled with like-minded old social activists and would find just the right people to go out on the picket line and demonstrate with. When I walked into the auditorium, I found people who looked like me—kind of recycled hippies who still wanted to give flowers to police officers. But they were really quiet, low-key—not a firebrand among them—and everyone's hair was clean. But there were plenty of beads and sandals, so I felt quite at home.

Thich Nhat Hanh stood at the center of the stage. He bowed to us, silently smiling. I bowed back—after all, I knew about *namaste* (even if I later found out that the bow was *gassho!*). I waited for something to happen. For what seemed like a very long time he just stayed quiet, gazing around at us, apparently trying to make eye contact with each person there. Eventually he spoke, and in his soft husky voice he told us that the best—the only— way to change the world was to change ourselves. For the next three hours he taught us concentration meditation. Afterward a Vietnamese nun whose home city had been destroyed by bombs spoke about her difficulty in letting go of anger over the devastation, sang a mournful song, then bowed to us. This was the end of the workshop, and the audience rose and left in silence, and I found myself weeping.

Everything Thich Nhat Hanh had said made sense to me, and I vowed to meditate every day. I went to AA meetings and announced to my friends that I had finally found the way I could best work the eleventh step. I talked a lot about peace. But the intention just didn't quite make it into action: I read and talked about meditation, but I didn't meditate. Finally a friend called me on this artificiality. I began to visit gatherings of the three major Buddhist traditions in the West the way I went through a cafeteria line: a little Zen as an appetizer, a little Tibetan as an entree, some Vipassana for dessert. In some ways this "tasting" was like exploring different kinds of AA meetings—speaker, discussion, Step, etc.—all over New York City. The formats were different, but the basic teachings were the same. I was attracted to Buddhism enough to keep seeking various teachers and events, but I wasn't really getting involved. I didn't have the Buddhist equivalent of an AA home group.

Another friend suggested that I read Joseph Goldstein and Jack Kornfield's *Seeking the Heart of Wisdom* because "it has exercises at the end of each chapter so maybe you'll get more engaged with the Dharma, the Buddha's teachings." I began the book and became totally caught up in it—so much so that I got into trouble with my partner the first week. I had just finished reading the chapter on nonharming; the mindfulness exercise was to raise awareness by not harming another living thing—animal or vegetable—for a week. Driving to the country that weekend, my partner announced, "This is the weekend we have to weed all the gardens."

"I can't," I replied, "I'm doing an exercise and I can't kill anything, even weeds, for a week."

"I know: you just want me to do all the yard work while you go off and climb a mountain."

In AA when we're having a bad day, we just decide to let go of what's been making us unhappy and emotionally start a new day right at that moment. So I started a new week that day and did my share of garden chores, mindfully.

About six months later, Insight Meditation teachers Joseph Goldstein and Sharon Salzberg held a three-day meditation workshop at a local college, and I went. I was miserable. Every joint and muscle was squealing and my mind was rat-a-tat gibberish. Joseph defined the word *insight* as seeing the way things really are, and my first insights had to do with the nature of mind and body—and were all negative. But I learned the basics of meditation and finally began to practice it.

I continued to read books about Buddhism and to meditate, but my practice really got off the ground when I went on my first silent meditation retreat at Insight Meditation Society in Barre, Massachusetts, founded by several teachers, including Goldstein and Salzberg, who had studied Buddhism at monasteries in Southeast Asia. Having the opportunity for continuity of practice without distractions, I began to have some small wisp of insight. When I sat to meditate, alone with my mind, I felt the same way I had the first time I tried to do a "fearless" inventory in AA. My insight into the nature of *my* mind was that there was some kind of committee of crazy beings living in my head who might not even be from this planet. The cascade of outrageous thoughts sometimes was so powerful that I felt terror or grief. In a flash, I could envision the next day or week or lifetime and would start to make concrete plans to make my vision come true.

I would have believed that I had gone around the bend if it hadn't been for a small-group interview with a teacher the second day of the retreat. It was the first retreat for all of us in that group, and much to my astonishment, my mental experiences had not been unique. As we shared, we discovered that we had all had the same types of physical and mental discomforts—and I was reminded of my early days in AA meetings when I found out how very common my drinking experiences and feelings about them had been.

The first riveting insight was that what I was seeing was not the nature of *my* mind but the nature of *the* mind. My particular mind is no more original than my alcoholism is. I knew by now that understanding the commonality of alcoholic experience could help me to stay sober, but I wasn't at all sure at first what I would gain from learning that there was some kind of uncontrollable nut living in my head—and everyone else's, which I had sometimes suspected before then.

Fortunately for me, I had a few more important insights: First, whatever formations (thoughts or emotions) the mind creates are impermanent—and sometimes so fleetingly so that I could barely grasp them. And second, there was much more to this Buddhism thing than I had imagined. I had gotten into it for all the physical and mental benefits of meditation and as a way to strengthen my working of Step Eleven, but I had found myself encountering . . . myself, in a way I had never known possible. I had begun to glimpse the possibility that the Buddha ("Awakened One") was somehow, somewhere inside *me*.

6

CHANGING
MY MIND

WHEN I WENT to AA, what I read in its literature was much less important to me than the intimate stories I heard people share about themselves in meetings. To the extent that I identified with their feelings rather than comparing the details of my experiences to theirs, I discovered the commonality of our lives and essentially joined the human race. Their honesty made my own possible. I learned to understand the AA program through the context of others' lives and recovery, including the cofounders, Bill W. and Dr. Bob S. I decided to try to do the same thing by learning something about the life of Siddhartha Gautama, the man who became the historical Buddha.

I knew from my first trip into relatively remote areas of Nepal that many aspects of the way of life had not changed significantly since Siddhartha was born in Lumbini, near the Indian border, in the sixth century BCE. On four subsequent trips to Nepal and India, I immersed myself as much as possible in the cultural continuities that might help me understand his life better.

Siddhartha was the son of the head of the Sakya clan and lived a life of privilege and protection. A seer had predicted before his birth that the son would become either a great political leader or a great spiritual leader. His father gave him every possible material enticement to ensure that Siddhartha would "come into the family business" as his heir. Despite having "everything"—palaces, dancing girls, a wife he loved, a newborn son—Siddhartha asked himself, "Is this all there is?"

Although I have no claims to royalty, growing up in a middle-class Western family and having all my material needs more than adequately answered I had found myself seeking some deeper meaning to life (often in a bottle) and asking myself the same question. Like other idealistic malcontents of my generation, I had become an adolescent expatriate, then a hippie, then a political activist, before becoming enmeshed—still kicking and screaming "peace"—in the Establishment. Siddhartha followed a path not out of the ordinary for his time and place: He turned his back on the bountiful life he was leading and sought among ascetic teachers in northern India answers to what it means to be born as a human being and to sicken, age, and die.

For twenty-nine years Siddhartha lived in luxury. For six years he was an ascetic spiritual wanderer. He had not found the answer to his spiritual quest through extremes, so he turned to what he called the Middle Path. On the night of his thirty-fifth birthday, while meditating near Bodhgaya, India, he became enlightened about the questions regarding the nature of life that had driven his search, and he spent the next forty-five years teaching others about the pervasiveness of suffering (*dukkha*), the causes of suffering, the fact that the end of suffering is possible, and the path that can lead to the end of suffering, teachings widely known as the Four Noble Truths.

Now called the Buddha (the "Enlightened One" or "Awakened One"), he specifically defined *dukkha* as aging, illness, death, sorrow, despair, not getting or losing what we cling to. (Although *dukkha* is translated variously as suffering, dis-ease, dissatisfaction, pain, or stress, I'll frequently use the original Pali term, with all its connotations.) I had no trouble acknowledging that life is filled with suffering—I had been depressive all my life. I could easily see that natural aspects of life, such as aging, illness, and death, cause pain. It took me a lot longer to understand that suffering originated with and was perpetuated when I, who am myself impermanent, cling to other things that are impermanent (life, health, a life partner, a job) as if they could ensure my happiness and would never change.

While I grappled with these ideas about clinging, I decided to turn to the Fourth Noble Truth—also called the Eightfold Path—to try to get a jump on the new happiness I was sure was coming my way. I just figured I'd work my linear way along the path until I too was enlightened. But I was quickly stymied. The more I learned about the Eightfold Path, the more certain I became that it should be called the Eightfold *Circle*. After even more study, it was clear to me that the only way to "lay out" the Eightfold Path was to use a hologram!—because only a three-dimensional rendering could show that everything is related to everything else.

Because the Eightfold Path falls into three broad areas—wisdom, morality, and mental training—I decided to start with the larger areas, beginning with mental training because that was my entry point into Buddhism, and because I'm perverse enough to want to master what I thought was the "ultimate goal" first.

Although I was able to meditate from the beginning, with all its benefits, I really didn't understand why I was meditating until I began to have insight into all the other teachings. Just as I had to start with Step One in AA, I found that I needed to start with the Four Noble Truths in Buddhism. And in what seemed like simple statements, I found a depth and complexity that challenged and intrigued me.

Only by patiently exploring the ideas could I assimilate them into my life and into my AA program. Only then could I integrate Twelve Steps into the Eightfold Path, the third part of this book. I had learned through people in AA that I had to change my way of living in the world if I was to be a "happy" recovering alcoholic. I was about to learn that I had to change my way of thinking about the world if I was to be happy. Period.

7

THE FIRST
NOBLE TRUTH

SUFFERING. The word itself conjured up all kinds of painful memories for me: Hangovers. Humiliations. Lost jobs. Accidents. Wrecked relationships. The Buddha sure had it right about the pervasiveness of dukkha. He stated clearly what dukkha is:

> Birth is suffering; ageing is suffering; sickness is suffering; death is suffering; sorrow, lamentation, pain, grief, and despair are suffering; not to obtain what one wants is suffering . . . [*The Middle-Length Discourses of the Buddha (Majjhima Nikaya)* 9.15]

But then he added: "in short, the *five aggregates* affected by clinging are suffering." I was with him until that point, but I had no idea what the "five aggregates" were or what they had to do with me. Out came the books again. This simple statement about suffering and the "aggregates" led me right into the most difficult concept in Buddhism for me and for many other people: *anatta*, or not-self.

NOT-SELF

Recently, when I introduced a new student of Buddhism to not-self, he whined, "Do we have to talk about this now? It's so complicated. And I don't agree with it anyway." I sincerely wished we didn't, but having at least a glancing understanding of *anatta* is the only way to get at the cause of suffering, in the Second Noble Truth.

Some of the misconceptions about Buddhism are that it's nihilistic and that it says we don't exist. It's not nihilistic, and what doesn't exist is a *permanent, unchanging, separate, autonomous anything* that can be called *self*. But, a small voice says, when I look in the mirror every morning, *I* am there, and when I see you walking down the street I can recognize you because *you* are there. True—relatively, conventionally speaking. *I* am recognizably there, and so are *you*. But what I see is not permanent or unchanging—if it were, children would never grow up and people would never age and die or even change their minds about anything. Ultimately, the conventional "self" I think I see is not an independent element *separate* from the so-called aggregates of which I am composed. And what are these aggregates?

- *Form, or matter*: all physical, material objects in the external world, including our bodies and sense organs
- *Feeling*: the affective experience of pleasant, unpleasant, or neither-pleasant-nor-unpleasant
- *Perception*: distinguishing through our sense organs the characteristics of beings and objects, involving and including recognition and memory
- *Mental formations*: all mental factors, such as thoughts and emotions
- *Consciousness*: awareness through one of the *six* sense organs (eye, ear, skin, nose, tongue, and—in Buddhist thinking—mind)

That is, our material form is not "self." Our experience of pleasant or unpleasant feelings is not self. Our perception of beings and objects is not self. Our awareness through sense organs is not self. Can we come up with any other component of our self that we can point to?

At this question, posed by the Buddha and many Buddhist teachers, my first reaction was to say, "Yes, a soul." But when challenged by Buddhist teachers to define *soul*, I had a knee-jerk response from the Judeo-Christian perspective of the culture in which I was raised: soul is a unique immaterial spiritual essence in each living being. But I certainly couldn't *point to* a soul or even objectively identify soul apart from the aggregates. At first, the search for the soul seemed like the kind of topic that I had last addressed in my college years, usually in the company of a lot of drinks.

In time, I began to realize that this notion of *anatta*—and the subsequent necessity of taking responsibility for my own life rather than relying on a Creator God to direct or forgive me—became one of the most attractive aspects of Buddhism for me. This deepening understanding led me back to closer examination of the aggregates.

When we look at the list of aggregates, none is permanent: Our *bodies* change as we age. Eating may *feel* very pleasant when we're very hungry, neither pleasant nor unpleasant if we're sated, or unpleasant if we've just overeaten—at least for a while, until we become hungry again. When we are *conscious*, we can recognize familiar objects and people when we encounter (*perceive*) them because of the element of memory that is part of consciousness. We can *think* about where we'd like to go on vacation and actually experience the *emotion* of excitement. When we (form) get into an elevator and smell (perception through sense gate because we are conscious) someone's heavy perfume, we may find the scent very unpleasant (feeling), but our sense of smell adapts quickly and we soon are not aware of the scent. Every aggregate is constantly changing.

So where does that leave *me*? Metaphorically, like a rainbow. When certain conditions of sunlight, temperature, and moisture occur simultaneously, we see a rainbow. When certain conditions of form, feeling, perception, mental formations, and consciousness come together, "I" see "myself" in the mirror. When weather conditions change dramatically, the rainbow fades. If someone turns off the light, I can no longer see my reflection. So this thing I experience as "I" is an ever-shifting confluence of impermanent components living in a universe of ever-changing components. As Zen priest Jisho Warner has described the phenomenon: "*I am an ever-changing river in an ever-changing river.*"

So *I* am a confluence of impermanent aggregates, and the Buddha said that "the five aggregates affected by clinging are suffering" because inherent in the word *clinging* is the sense of grasping something as if it will never change or go away. To revisit the mirror, when I perceive my image I may suffer for a time because there's a zit on my nose (material form) or I'm having a bad hair day and I'm depressed that others will think I'm ugly (mental formations). But this reaction too will pass, eventually, when the zit goes away or I style my hair. Unfortunately, I find it much harder to let go of other clung-to ideas or objects or people as easily as to an aspect of my not-self even though at some level I know that they too consist of impermanent aggregates affected by changing conditions.

In some Buddhist traditions, such as Zen, the phenomenon of not-self is called emptiness: We are empty of a separate, permanent, autonomous self. Particle physicists have explained that objects are made up of cells and molecules and that all are equally empty of a "self" if they are examined under a powerful microscope. Somehow it seems easier to realize that a table is "empty" than that we are. Yet we—being empty and impermanent—so often put all our hearts and minds into clinging to a car, a house, or another person that is equally empty. In this creation of a sense of self through clinging, we set into action the mechanisms that generate *dukkha*. Joseph Goldstein once summed it up this way: "If there's anyone home to suffer, they will."

8

THE SECOND
AND THIRD
NOBLE TRUTHS

BEFORE I GOT SOBER, more mornings than I like to remember I woke up with the thought "Oh, no. I did it again." *It* was another night of drinking, of half-remembered humiliations, of driving home with one eye closed so there would be only one center stripe on the road, of throwing up and, still dressed, passing out on my bed—not always alone. I never meant for any of these things to happen. I would just stop for one drink after work with friends or plan to have one glass of wine with dinner or order one beer when everyone else at the ballgame did. But so often—not every time, but too often—everything seemed to spiral out of my control and I'd end up drunk again and up to my neck in *dukkha* that I had created for myself. I just couldn't figure out how I kept getting myself into the same kind of fix. I was intelligent, well educated, successful in business—why did I keep doing this to myself?

The cofounders of AA would answer, "Because you're an alcoholic." This is true, but I longed for a more complete explanation for why I kept repeating the same actions and expecting different outcomes. I found a clarification that helped me to understand the dynamics of the process in the Four Noble Truths. "Dr. Buddha," in the metaphor of the physician who has diagnosed the illness (*dukkha*) in the First Noble Truth, described the origin of *dukkha* in the Second Noble Truth:

It is craving, which . . . is accompanied by delight and lust . . . that is, craving for sensual pleasures . . . . [*The Middle-Length Discourses of the Buddha (Majjhima Nikaya)* 9.16]

And he clarified the cessation of *dukkha* in the Third Noble Truth:

It is the remainderless fading away and ceasing, the giving up, relinquishing, letting go, and rejecting of that same craving. [*The Middle-Length Discourses of the Buddha (Majjhima Nikaya)* 9.17]

For me one of the popular definitions of alcoholism as a physical compulsion and a mental obsession fit perfectly into the Buddha's description of the dynamics of craving. Taking the first drink triggered a physiological need for more alcohol that was painfully insistent and almost impossible to ignore. When I needed a drink, I felt physically ill and could think of nothing else. I manipulated people and circumstances any way I could to get a drink. It was the craving for what alcohol did to and for me that kept me in *dukkha*, and I had to stop drinking alcohol to end that particular form of *dukkha*, which we will explore in more detail in Chapter 10. But what happens when beings are able to completely relinquish all craving? Nirvana.

NIRVANA

Popular culture tends to describe nirvana as a place (like Heaven or Hawaii), but the original word—*nirvana* in Sanskrit, *nibbana* in Pali—means the "extinction" or "cessation" of that craving/ desire/clinging, as well as of other related "defilements" that impact suffering: hatred/aversion and delusion/illusion. That is, nirvana is the condition of nondesire, nonaversion, and nondelusion. For me, as an alcoholic, in a very relative sense, I seek cessation from the craving for alcohol and from the mental obsession with drinking.

I have never personally known anyone who achieved nirvana as a permanent state, but I and many others I know have experienced fleeting moments of extraordinary freedom—freedom from, freedom to. Such moments—riding a horse, reading a book, painting a picture, dancing—have been so perfectly in the present moment that I have not experienced desire, aversion, or delusion. Within this great sense of freedom, I have felt relief, lightness, and remarkable happiness. But nirvana doesn't just happen, and neither does this freedom. We need to understand the dynamics of how we develop craving, hatred, and delusion and be willing to take the path to end them: the Eightfold Path of the Fourth Noble Truth, in the next chapter. Before we can get rid of these problems, we need to understand the Buddha's explanation of how they come to be such a resolute part of our experience.

DEPENDENT ORIGINATION

The Buddha explained how *dukkha* arises through a complex (circular) scheme known as the *twelve links of dependent origination*. Note that several of these links were introduced earlier in our discussion of the aggregates and not-self:

1. Ignorance, which leads to
2. Mental formations (thoughts and emotions), which lead to
3. Consciousness, which requires
4. Material form, which has
5. Six sense gates, through which stimuli generate
6. Contact, sense impressions that generate
7. Feelings of pleasant, unpleasant, or neither-pleasant-nor-unpleasant that generate
8. Desire or craving (or dislike), which causes
9. Grasping or attachment (or aversion), which generates
10. Becoming (being), which generates
11. Birth, which is the condition for
12. *Dukkha.*

Going through this list from 1 to 12 explains how everything originates dependent upon the conditions that preceded it. With a lot of study I found this explanation elegant—but always daunting.

For the purposes of this book, we can turn to the Buddha's simpler summaries of dependent origination (this may seem less clear initially, but read on!):

- When *this* exists, *that* exists.
- When *this* arises, *that* arises.
- When *this* does not exist, *that* does not exist.
- When *this* ceases, *that* ceases.

Let's look at just a few of these links as they come up in everyday life, using a common example:

- Material form. I (my body and mind) go into a movie theater.
- Six sense gates. As I walk past the concession stand, I see popcorn.
- Sense impressions. I smell the freshly popped, hot buttered popcorn.
- Feelings. The smell is very pleasant.
- Desire or craving. I want some popcorn.
- Grasping or attachment. I buy and eat all of a large box of popcorn. Even though I'm so full I'm uncomfortable (*dukkha*), I want more popcorn (attachment).

Or (remembering that mind is a sense gate):

- When *this* (perception of popcorn) exists, *that* (desire for popcorn) exists.
- When *this* (perception of popcorn) arises, *that* (desire for popcorn) arises.
- When *this* (perception of popcorn) does not exist, *that* (desire for popcorn) does not exist.

- When *this* (perception of popcorn) ceases, *that* (desire for popcorn) ceases.

What becomes evident in this simple scheme is that when we can interrupt the links at any point, we break the chain leading to grasping and *dukkha*. But before I got sober, if I saw, smelled, tasted, touched (a cold can of beer), heard (a vendor at a game calling out, "Beer!"), or thought about a drink, I took it. I didn't know I could interrupt the craving that arose.

Paraphrasing dependent origination in the language often heard at AA meetings: "Everything that ever happened in the world had to have happened for me to be here, in this chair, today." I may ask, "What does my having a cup of tea at an AA meeting have to do with everything that ever happened in the world?" Answering that question would fill the rest of this book and more, but let's consider a few of the things that had to happen for me to be drinking this cup of tea.

- The tea plant had to have sun, air, much moisture, well-drained earth, and climatic warmth to grow.
- Someone in prehistoric India or China had to discover that boiling (which depends on fire) tea leaves in water produces a potable, salutary beverage.
- The Dutch East India Company had to introduce tea to Europe, thereby opening trade between Asia and Europe.
- My ancestors had to come to North America and start the Revolutionary War at the Boston Tea Party.
- Bill W. and Dr. Bob had to found AA.
- The popularity of tea as a caffeinated beverage had to grow so much that it—along with coffee—is served at most AA meetings.

- A very long line of individuals had to plant, cultivate, harvest, package, ship, purchase, prepare, and serve this particular tea. They all had to have food, shelter, medicine, etc., . . .
- I have to be here to drink it (and have food, shelter, medicine, etc., . . . and have sought out recovery in AA), and it will eventually cause me discomfort in the need to urinate and having insomnia from the caffeine.

Then there's the cup—the history of ceramics since prehistory, the building I'm in, the community where I live, and so on end-lessly. All for a cup of tea, or anything else in our world, because *everything* is interrelated and thus depends on the causes and con-ditions of everything else to exist. There is no way that we can go back and change Indian or European or American or even our own personal history. But at any moment, we can change our *future* by breaking a link of the chain of dependent origination.

Consider our simple example with a few places where the link can be broken:

- I walk up to the beverage station, see a newly opened box of black tea, think about how good it would taste, and want a cup of it. But I remember that black tea is so heavily caffeinated that I'll have trouble sleeping, and I choose instead an herbal tea. (Here the first sense gate is eye, but the mind sense gate is also open because I'm conscious, and memory tells me both how the black tea will taste and what the black tea will do to me. I see that other teas are offered. I make the choice—break the link of desire—and drink an herbal tea.)

- Or I go through all the steps in the above example and sit down. When I taste the herbal tea, I find the flavor unpleasant in the extreme. I dump the tea and pour myself a cup of coffee because I really wanted coffee in the first place and would rather have insomnia than drink that awful brew of sticks and leaves. (As is always the case, I've created my own *dukkha* through desire/aversion, perhaps even with the delusion that this time will be different—my delusion of choice as an active alcoholic—and I'll be able to sleep.)

All of these examples, complex and simple, are premised on causality, on cause and effect, on *karma*.

KARMA

Karma, quite simply, is volitional action. The "law of karma" is that *every* volitional action has consequences to ourselves and to others. Nothing is ever lost. Karma has nothing to do with the kind of doom and destiny that is described as karma in much popular culture—nothing is preordained *except by our own volitional actions*. But for an alcoholic, the karmic doom we risk when we pick up a drink is well reflected in a saying heard in AA: "One drink is too many but a thousand isn't enough." If we pick up the first drink, we trigger the compulsion to drink, which cannot be satisfied and so keeps us drinking.

A useful metaphor for describing karma is a seed: Whatever kind of seed we plant will determine the kind of fruit we get—at the time and place that the particular seed needs for fruition. If we put a lettuce seed into the proper soil, we will get a lettuce plant in that variety's germination time. If we plant a redwood seed, we will get a redwood tree when the seed germinates—which may be a wait of several hundred years because the temperature of a forest fire is needed for redwood germination.

If we consistently act toward others with anger, we are sowing the seeds of anger in ourselves, and when conditions in the future are right, anger will be expressed. On the other hand, if we act with compassion, we sow the seeds of kindness. The Bible acknowledges this in the saying "What you sow, so shall you reap."

The Buddha made a similar statement in numerous places that has become part of a daily morning chant in many Buddhist monasteries:

> All beings are the owners of their karma,
> heirs of their karma,
> born of their karma,
> related to their karma,
> Supported by their karma.

When we realize that all social conventions and laws are the products of human's thoughts/intentions, we can see that in addition to personal karma, there is family karma, community karma, corporate karma, national karma, even global karma. Knowing this, many Buddhists are moved to become social activists, to try to break the dependent links that cause injustice and suffering in the world.

When we look for the origin and cessation of personal suffering, we find them in the interplay of the aggregates of which we are composed, the factors of dependent origination, and the law of karma. To find our way through this complex interplay, the Buddha outline a specific path we could follow to end *dukkha*: the Fourth Noble Truth, the Eightfold Path, Chapter 9.

9

THE FOURTH
NOBLE TRUTH

THE FOURTH NOBLE TRUTH consists of the Eightfold Path leading to happiness and freedom. Like the links of dependent origination, if any part of the path is missing, the rest cannot be realized. That is, to fulfill the eightfold circle, one must understand and practice all of the steps/stages/links. For convenience, we'll follow the scheme in which the eight are often considered within the three groups of wisdom, morality, and mental discipline:

THE EIGHTFOLD PATH

Wisdom Teachings
- Wise Understanding
- Wise Thought

Morality Teachings
- Wise Speech
- Wise Action
- Wise Livelihood

Mental Discipline Teachings
- Wise Effort
- Wise Mindfulness
- Wise Concentration

WISDOM TEACHINGS

Wise understanding consists primarily of comprehending the teachings we took up in the preceding chapter: the Four Noble Truths, impermanence, not-self, dependent origination, and karma. The understanding teachings are basic to everything in Buddhism and are closely related to wise thought, also sometimes known as wise intention or wise aspiration to distinguish the word *thought* from its most common connotations. When we understand the nature of suffering, its cause, and its cessation, we realize that we are interrelated with all beings and that all our mental formations (thoughts and emotions) and actions have an effect on ourselves and others. When we understand this "perfectly"—to use the Buddha's word—we then can see how very critical our thoughts and intentions are. For this reason, he defined wise thought as "the thought of renunciation, the thought of non-ill-will, the thought of harmlessness."

In this teaching, we thus are to renounce thoughts/intentions of harming in any form. The Buddha emphasized the importance of such renunciation in the collection of poems known as the *Dhammapada* by stressing that through our actions and through our thoughts/intentions we shape our worlds. In Pali, the language of the Buddha's teachings, the same word, *citta*, means both "mind" and "heart." Here's how one modern teacher, Thanissaro Bhikkhu, translates two verses from the very first poem in the *Dhammapada*:

> Phenomena are preceded by the heart [mind],
> Ruled by the heart,
> Made of the heart.
> If you speak or act with a corrupted heart,
> Then suffering follows you—as the wheel of the cart,
> The track of the ox
> That pulls it.
> . . .
> Hostilities aren't stilled
> Through hostility, regardless.
> Hostilities are stilled
> Through non-hostility:
> This, an unending truth.

When we thoroughly understand that our thoughts/intentions result in our karmic inheritance as surely as a cart track follows an ox, we come to the practical insight of seeing into things as they really are: hatred never ends by hatred, only by love—and testimony to this "unending truth" can be found throughout the history of violence and wars, which, even when won, cause so much suffering. We can also see that each time an alcoholic drinks, he or she is asking for unavoidable *dukkha*, as we will discuss in detail in Part Three.

MORALITY TEACHINGS

The morality teachings of wise speech, action, and livelihood acknowledge the role of the wisdom teachings in our everyday life. Unquestionably wise understanding and thought are necessary for us to live in a way that causes harm to no one, the essence of the morality teachings.

Wise speech encompasses avoiding lying, slander, abusive speech, and frivolous speech such as gossip. For many people, it is by far the most challenging part of practicing the teachings of the Eightfold Path. How many times have we said, "I wish I hadn't said that," or even "I wish I *had* said that," because within the context of nonharming, keeping silent can abet harming when injustices exist. We can often identify lying when we are telling a falsehood to someone else, but it may be harder to catch ourselves when we lie to ourselves or exaggerate or minimize something to make a story—or ourselves—seem better, or even worse.

Similarly, when we gossip, we often build ourselves up at others' expense, if not by putting them down at least by seeming self-important. An interesting spiritual practice is to make a commitment for twenty-four hours not to talk about anyone who is not present. It can really cut down on what we find to talk about and raise our consciousness about how much of our speech is gossip.

Using abusive language—loud, crude, profane—separates us from others and "plants seeds" of abusiveness, anger, and aversion in us. What it says about our heart/minds is sometimes shocking, especially when what comes out of our mouths reflects a bias against against a group because of age, race, size, or any other criteria that cause us to perceive others as different. We may be unconscious of a prejudice against, let us say, short men until one makes us angry and we shout, "Well, look at the banty rooster strut!" We will continue to be unaware unless we cultivate the habit of listening to ourselves speak and make a conscious decision to eliminate such language.

All types of wrong speech—whether lying, exaggerating, gossiping, or cursing—result in our creating a concrete sense of self, isolated from other beings, defying interconnectedness and impermanence, as well as having karmic effects on others. Wise speech is both true and useful and is spoken with kindness at an appropriate time.

Wise action recognizes the karmic inheritance of all actions for ourselves and for others and, simply put, is action that does not harm anyone (including ourselves) in any way. All the world's religions have codes of behavior and judge actions as being "right" or "wrong," "good" or "bad," or "moral" or "immoral." These terms are extremely judgmental and don't acknowledge the effects of karma. In contrast, Buddhism describes actions that cause *dukkha* as *unskillful* and those that promote happiness as *skillful*. Inherent in this scheme is the understanding that truly happy people do not voluntarily do things that harm others and at the same time themselves, ever. Think for a moment about road rage: When we are caught up in greed (wanting to go faster), hatred (of other drivers in our way), and delusion (that we're entitled to drive the way we want to), we will do unskillful things that harm (sometimes fatally) others and ourselves. With wise understanding and intention, we will try to avoid causing anyone harm, even in traffic jams and on freeways.

Although the earliest monks had many rules to live by, the Buddha specifically laid out just a few guidelines for householders. Rather than describing these Five Precepts as rules, he said that they were *training* precepts based on the way an enlightened being would act. If we want to be like an enlightened one, then we should practice the Five Precepts in a way so that our behavior will always elicit approval from "the wise ones." The Five Precepts fit within the Eightfold Path much as a small Russian nesting doll fits within a larger one—they look alike but one is slightly scaled down. Here are the training principles for laypeople:

1. Avoid harming or killing other beings. This precept resonates with and summarizes all the points made about nonharming in the wise action step of the Eightfold Path.

2. Avoid taking what is not freely given. Basically, this means to not steal, but when we use the phrase *what is not freely given*, we can see that this precept is very broad indeed. It encompasses things such as exploitation of natural resources by the few; slavelike labor practices; and sexual harassment, especially of people over whom one has power through wealth, age, position, or physical strength. Whenever we take what is not freely given, we are acting out of greed, one of the primary factors causing *dukkha*.

3. Avoid sexual misconduct. *Misconduct* means "unskillful conduct" so we should refrain from any sexual behavior that harms another. In contemporary terms, we avoid sexual activity

outside of committed relationship if we or the other person is in one.

4. Avoid harmful speech. Unskillful speech, the opposite of wise speech, is untrue, slanderous, frivolous, abusive, unkind, ill-timed, or frequently all of the above if we're drunk.

5. Avoid intoxicants that dull the mind. This is not a prohibition against ever having a drink but a recognition that abusive use of intoxicants dulls the mind, resulting in harmful—often violent—acts toward others, the antithesis of the clear-headed mindfulness that is our goal (for this reason, some Buddhists do not drink at all).

As a recovering alcoholic, I was astonished that although there were only five "commandments" handed down 2,600 years ago, one of the five had to do with abusing alcohol and drugs. Whether we are alcoholics or not, when we violate the fifth precept and reach the state that our minds are dulled by intoxicants, we are very likely to violate some or all of the other four precepts.

Wise livelihood at first seems fairly evident: don't earn a living by harming others as weapons dealers, drug dealers, killers of living beings, or thieves. But the distinctions between skillful livelihood and unskillful may not always be clear-cut. Among the very many "hidden" sources of unskillful livelihood are selling goods and services by people who are treated inhumanely, dealing in products that harm the environment, commissioning through purchases products that harm, and receiving dividends from investments—often unknowingly in an IRA or portfolio—in corporations that harm beings and the environment.

Wise livelihood encompasses not only where we gain income but also how we relate with others in our workplace. Realizing that unskillful speech and actions can harm others, we can commit ourselves to becoming more skillful in our interactions in the workplace, the community, our own homes. But this commitment cannot be fulfilled by a snap decision—it takes intention and effort and practice to develop the wise and compassionate mind that leads to wise and compassionate action.

MENTAL DISCIPLINE
TEACHINGS

Understanding in our heart/minds that our intentions create our world, we become willing to develop mindfulness in the present moment, which is a necessary condition for living a life of non-harming. Wise effort, mindfulness, and concentration thus give us the skills we need to learn to have a happy life and to turn off the "automatic pilots" that mindlessly create so much "bad" karma. Many people who turn to meditation and other mental disciplines frequently do so to have a "bliss trip" that has the quality of unreality to it. In real Buddhist practice, meditation practices may have some lovely side effects (lower blood pressure, ability to handle stress, serenity), but the emphasis is on a happiness based in reality rather than escapism.

It is said that the Buddha gave more talks about wise effort than any other subject. This isn't really surprising, because developing mental discipline, just like physical training in any sport, only happens when we are willing to put in the time and energy needed to hone our skills. The intended outcome recognizes that practice develops skills that we can use in the wider world. For example, many athletes regularly spend hours doing aerobic exercises and working with weights—not so that they can go out and climb stairs or lift weights in public but so that they will have greater endurance and strength when they play basketball, tennis, football, baseball, or any other sport. Classical singers spend hours doing scales—not so that they can walk out on a stage and sing scales but so that their voices will be stronger and more flexible when they sing opera, sacred music, or lieder. Meditators practice daily meditation—not so that they can sit silently in public but so that they can act with mindful awareness in their everyday life. It is mindfulness that buys us the time and heart/mind space to *respond* with wisdom and compassion rather than *reacting* with greed, anger, and delusion to the situations that we live through in all our waking moments.

MEDITATION INSTRUCTIONS

Mental discipline starts with intention and happens through effort. We must intend to take the time for ourselves every day— even if only for five or ten minutes—to pause, in silence, and concentrate our minds. Different Buddhist traditions practice mental discipline—meditation—in a variety of ways. Almost all have two components: concentration and insight. We concentrate our minds by single-pointed focus on an object, a word or sound, a vision, or most commonly our breath. We sit (meditate) for a predetermined amount of time. After our minds are concentrated, we open spaciously to observe whatever comes up in our minds, which leads to insight, to seeing things as they are. Simple, yes. Easy, no.

Here are simplified meditation instructions:

Sit in a chair or cross-legged on a cushion in a position that you can comfortably hold for ten minutes or longer. Sit erectly but not stiffly. Let your hands fold in your lap or rest on your thighs. Let your eyes gently close. Scan your body for any areas of tension, and "breathe into" any tight spots you find to relieve the tension. "Invite" your breath into your body and begin to observe—not control—your breathing. Notice where you feel your breath most strongly—your nostrils, chest, or abdomen—and that place becomes your single point of focus.

Don't follow your breath in and out the whole way through your respiratory system, but observe it closely as it passes that one spot. Is it shallow or deep? Coarse or smooth? Is the air cooler when it comes in than when it goes out? If another object of attention—sound, pain, thinking—becomes predominant, let your attention rest on it as it arises and passes away, then focus again on your inhalations and exhalations.

Now here's what really happens:

You sit self-consciously in a chair, trying so hard to hold very still that your whole body is stiff. Already the chair feels too hard and you wish you had chosen a cushion instead. You begin to watch your breath, feeling as if there's a cinch around your chest, and you strain to take in enough air, sort of claustrophobic. By the third breath, your mind is off and running: *This is so boring. I didn't get enough sleep last night and could just nod out right now. I am so uncomfortable. My back hurts. My nose itches. I will scratch it. Now my arm itches. The itch is moving. This can't be doing me any good. I'd be better off going to a yoga class. Maybe I should take a vacation in India and go to an ashram. They probably only eat vegetarian food there, so I'd better be prepared to give up the burgers. I'm hungry right now. I wonder how long I've been sitting here? Oh, no, only three minutes.*

Congratulations! You've just had a *very normal* meditation experience and seen how out of control your mind is, left to its own devices (somewhat analogous to what happens when we're in a blackout, except that we can't remember the mental events). This mind is no different from the way it usually is, but most of the time we are not at all in touch with what our minds are doing. Only when we sit down to observe the mind do we begin to get an inkling of how it works most of the time.

THE FIVE HINDRANCES

Each time we meditate is a microcosm of life itself, and the things that derail us from simple focus on our breath—called the Five Hindrances—occur throughout our everyday lives. When we are not aware of what's happening, the mind that creates our world can push us around a lot. The hindrances are as follows:

1. Desire. In the example above, desire for a "good" meditation experience, then to end an itch, then to have a hamburger.
2. Aversion (to the uncomfortable chair, the itch). Dislike (emotional states of irritation, anger, hatred).
3. Restlessness. Physically, moving to avoid discomfort. Mentally, planning.
4. Sloth and torpor. Sleepiness, boredom, lethargy.
5. Doubt. "This is the wrong practice for me."

These hindrances are chameleons—they change colors and reappear throughout our meditation time and time again. With practice—and wise effort—we recognize them increasingly quickly, gently bring our attention back to our breath, and calm our mind. Then we can begin to have insights into our reality: We are constantly inclined to move to avoid discomfort. The breath arises and passes away, impermanent, like everything. Sounds arise and pass away, impermanent, like everything. Our thoughts, our feelings, even our physical pains—the aggregates—arise and pass away, impermanent, like everything. Through meditation, to quote the Serenity Prayer, we enhance "the wisdom to know the difference" between skillful and unskillful thoughts and actions. We can increasingly develop the wisdom and the compassion to live with the impermanence of "One Day at a Time" and be joyous in our sobriety.

Part Three:

We

"I am We."

10

THE FOUR
SOBER TRUTHS:
ALCOHOLISM IS
DUKKHA

THE NATURE, CAUSE, and cessation of suffering are star-
tlingly clear when we revisit the Buddha's account of *dukkha* in the
Four Noble Truths and highlight its parallels to alcoholism.
According to the Buddha in the Four Noble Truths, suffering is
"the five aggregates affected by clinging"; the origin is craving; the
end is rejecting and letting go of craving; and the way to let go is
the Eightfold Path. The "Four Sober Truths" are that alcoholism is

a threefold disease that affects us physically, mentally, and spiritually; the disease is activated by drinking alcohol; it can only be ended by abstinence; and the path to abstinence is the Twelve Steps.

Much research into alcoholism has established that there is a physical, probably genetic, predisposition for the disease—it seems to run in families. Those of us who have this disease manifest characteristics of a physical addiction to and a mental obsession with drinking: craving, clinging—we are ensnared in *dukkha*.

When I first went to AA and asked how I could have possibly become an alcoholic, one man answered, "You're like a cucumber: If you dip a cucumber into brine, then pull it out, then dip it in again and keep doing that, eventually when you pull it out it's a pickle. And once it's a pickle, it will never be a cucumber again. You dipped into the bottle enough times that you're a pickle. You'll never be a cucumber again." The more I learned about alcoholism and the clearer I became about my own drinking behavior, the harder it was for me to understand why I repeatedly drank so much that I became a pickle. Finally, when I seriously studied the Buddha's teachings, the answer became obvious: The theory of dependent origination plainly explains why I drank myself into physical addiction and mental obsession, even as I denied that I had a problem. Even as I kept trying, unsuccessfully, to stop drinking.

THE DEPENDENT ORIGINATION
OF DRUNK *DUKKHA*

Parts of the scheme of dependent origination related to the five aggregates were obvious from the beginning of my drinking:

- I never intended to get drunk in social situations (ignorance), but I thought I could just have a few drinks and a good time (mental formations).
- I imagined how much fun I would have (consciousness) when someone invited me to a party.
- I (material form) would go to a party.
- I would see (sense gate) that everyone was drinking and having a good time.
- Someone would hand me a drink and I'd take the first sip (contact).
- A pleasant feeling would envelop me (feeling).
- I would want more of that feeling, more to drink (craving).
- I would have one drink after another (clinging) until I was drunk (being), throwing up, in a blackout, and humiliating myself.
- I would get sober and swear to never let that kind of behavior happen again, but I would go to another party ("rebirth") as soon as there was an opportunity.
- The whole cycle of drunkeness would play out again, perhaps this time with an automobile accident or an ended friendship. The realization that I "had done it again" made me despair (*dukkha*).

Talk about reruns—I played out the same scenario time after time after time, and nothing ever changed. When I went to AA, people told me to avoid people, places, and things that made me want to drink. That meant, for a start, not taking my material form to parties, bars, or any occasions where the primary activity would be drinking and where my eyes, nose, ears, and mind would be sense gates that could lead me to drink. Perhaps the most critical link was to avoid contact with alcohol—to not take that first drink, which would trigger craving and binging by activating the physical disease. And because the mind is a sense gate, whenever I allowed myself to obsess about drinking, I would set off the mental part of the disease.

When we recast some of the Buddha's simpler statements about dependent origination, active alcoholism is a perfect fit *for the alcoholic*:

> When *this* [contact with alcohol] exists, *that* [active alcoholism] exists.
> When *this* [contact with alcohol] arises, *that* [active alcoholism] arises.
> When *this* [contact with alcohol] does not exist, *that* [active alcoholism] does not exist.
> When *this* [contact with alcohol] ceases, *that* [active alcoholism] ceases.

AA members phrase the principles of dependent origination this way:

> If you don't drink, you won't get drunk.

Or

> It's the first drink that gets you drunk.

"If you don't drink, you won't get drunk" seemed simplistically obvious, even if I didn't realize for quite a while that it was factually accurate only if you are an alcoholic. The statement was not true for nonalcoholics, but it had never occurred to me that most people have only one or two drinks and don't get drunk. This blindness was part of my denial of my own alcoholism. I kept insisting, even to myself, that I could drink just like anyone else.

I argued a lot about the second phrase, about the first drink getting me drunk, and insisted that it was the fifth or fifteenth drink. Only when I began to understand the physically addictive aspect of alcoholism could I grasp the notion that if I didn't pick up the first drink, I wouldn't *have* to pick up the fifth or fifteenth. In terms of dependent origination, the first drink set off the craving for the second, which set off the craving for the third, . . . fifth, . . . fifteenth.

The only time I ever had just the first drink was when physical or social circumstances made it impossible for me to have the second. If I anticipated that how much I could drink might be limited by a situation, I tried to compensate: I would drink before I went and arrive high, I would bring wine with me as a "gift" that I could ensure would be opened, or I simply wouldn't go at all. No matter how many excuses I made up—"You can't have a party without a drink," "You'd drink too if you had my problems," "I can stop any time I want to"—the reality was that I *needed* to drink, that I had no choice.

KARMA IN A BOTTLE

The need for alcohol—which the fetters of denial hid from me— was a fact of my daily life for two decades and controlled my intentions, decisions, and actions—my karma—during the years I drank. With 20/20 hindsight, I can see the pattern clearly, and I'm amazed that I couldn't perceive what was happening at the time.

Alcoholism ruled many small things—choice of restaurants, which parties to attend, even which movies to go to (some lasted longer than I was willing to go without a drink)—but it also dictated some of my most important decisions. During the drunken decades, I got into two long relationships (one for ten years, one for five), both while I was quite drunk, and they ended because of alcoholism. I twice moved from New York to California and back—what AA members call a geographic cure—because I was sure everything would be better somewhere else. I took jobs that I really didn't want "to maintain my lifestyle" and got pressured out of them because I couldn't "live up to my potential" (hangovers have that effect). And on three occasions I made suicide attempts that should have killed me.

Our minds shape our worlds, but I didn't know that an addicted, neurotic mind was directing all my actions. Whenever I drank, I kept thinking that "This time will be different," but it never was. I just kept planting karmic seeds of self-destruction until they came to fruition and I tried to kill myself. Although I would have sworn that my drinking never hurt anyone but myself, I left enormous suffering in my wake, affected many other lives, and caused so much pain to those who loved me, through my suicide attempts, long absences, ruined relationships. My bottle-fed karma was to suffer and to hurt others, because that's the way I created it.

SOBER KARMA

The Third Noble Truth states that the cessation of *dukkha* is "the giving up, relinquishing, letting go, and rejecting" of craving. Although there is no way to change the unskillful karma we generated while we were drinking, living mindfully in sobriety enables us to change our karma for the future. We stop planting the seeds of deluded self-destructiveness, anger, shame, cruelty, and so on, and instead plant seeds of clarity and kindness, which will come to fruition if we stay sober. As one Buddhist teacher put it, "Good karma wears out the effects of old bad karma."

That great philosopher Woody Allen once said that 80 percent of life is simply showing up. While I was drinking, my material form usually showed up, but not much else. In sobriety, I am really here, and the rewards are astonishing. I know where I am. I know what I'm doing. I can remember what I've done—and I can learn from my experiences because I can remember them. All of this together means that my brain and heart are truly bonded and I can act with wisdom and compassion toward myself and others, whether I'm volunteering in a prison or rehabilitation center, participating as a responsible citizen in my community, or starting both a meditation group to share the Dharma and an AA meeting in an isolated community where neither existed.

ROADMAP FOR SOBRIETY

The cofounders of AA laid out a clear description of living sober, which involved avoiding some things (drinking, going into drinking situations) and actively doing other things (going to meetings; letting go of people, places, and things that made us want to drink; working the steps; placing our trust in a Higher Power).

Just as AA is an action program, so too within Buddhism there are actions, or tasks, for each of the Four Noble Truths:

1. For *dukkha*, our task is to understand it.
2. For the origin of *dukkha*, our task is to eliminate it.
3. For the end of *dukkha*, our task is to realize it.
4. For the path to the end of *dukkha*, our task is to follow it steadfastly.

To recast these statements in terms of alcoholism for the alcoholic:

1. For *alcoholism*, our task is to understand that it is a threefold disease.
2. For the origin of *alcoholism*, our task is to eliminate it by not taking the first drink.
3. For the end of *alcoholism*, our task is to realize sobriety.
4. For the path to the end of *alcoholism*, our task is to follow the Twelve Steps steadfastly.

At my first AA meeting, one of the ways I fed my denial was to be ruthlessly judgmental about things like the punctuation in the Twelve Steps and Twelve Traditions "window shades" and what I thought were inane slogans. Eventually, I reached the other extreme and did not want a word or a comma in AA literature changed even if it was incorrect.

One of the blessings of continuous sobriety and unwavering Buddhist practice has been to learn to monitor my "judging mind" and be more willing to accept the AA slogan *Live and Let Live*. My only alternative was to make others' lives unpleasant by perpetually pointing out their flaws to them, which is unskillful in the extreme.

11

TAKING SOBER REFUGE IN THE STEPS

In Alcoholics Anonymous, alcoholism is self-diagnosed, and attendance at meetings is voluntary, with no membership lists or dues. I am an alcoholic and a member of AA if I say I am. In much the same way, I am Buddhist and a follower of the Buddha's teachings if I say I am. In both instances, I have found a spiritual home where I can take refuge.

SOBER REFUGE

During the Buddha's lifetime, if someone wanted to formally become a follower of the Buddha, she or he would kneel before an ordained disciple and three times repeat phrases known as the Three Refuges, or in the Mahayana traditions as the Three Jewels or Three Treasures:

> I go for refuge to the Buddha.
> I go for refuge to the Dharma.
> I go for refuge to the Sangha.

Originally, going for refuge to the Buddha literally meant seeking sanctuary with that particular person, the man called Buddha. Going for refuge to the Dharma implied finding a safe haven in the Buddha's teachings. Going for refuge to the Sangha meant seeking security in the ordained spiritual community of the Buddha's followers. These meanings are still acknowledged today, but many Buddhists have expanded them, sometimes a little, sometimes a lot.

Buddha still refers to the enlightened man Siddhartha Gautama, but the term may also connote each one of us, because we have the potential to realize our own Buddha-nature, our personal awakening. The Buddha was not a god—he was a human being, just like we are, and he showed us that it was possible for each of us to awaken.

Dharma as a proper noun originally specifically meant the Buddha's teachings, but it also meant—and means—the Truth.

When Siddhartha achieved enlightenment, he did not invent the Truth; he discovered what had always been Truth and he taught it throughout his life: the Four Noble Truths, impermanence, not-self, dependent origination, and the law of karma.

The *Sangha* was originally the Buddha's ordained spiritual community, but today the word may be used to include all monastics and laypeople who follow the Buddha's teachings and practices. In the extreme, a few people today may use the term for all beings on their spiritual path—including animals.

The word *refuge* is especially interesting because it connotes some inner or outer danger from which we seek protection. Every day when I sit down to meditate, I first repeat the Three Refuges as a Buddhist and as a sober alcoholic. Here's what they mean to me:

I go for refuge to the Buddha, *to my own possibility for freedom and happiness as long as I do not drink.*

I go for refuge to the Dharma, *the possibility to see what is real and true in sobriety.*

I go for refuge to the Sangha, *to my interconnectedness with all beings and especially with other sober alcoholics.*

TAKING SOBER STEPS

Today, the broad connotations of *Buddha*, *Dharma*, and *Sangha* are treasured facets of how I work with AA's Twelve Steps. Here is the way I see the Twelve Steps through my Buddhist lens.

STEP ONE: WE ADMITTED WE WERE POWERLESS OVER ALCOHOL—THAT OUR LIVES HAD BECOME UNMANAGEABLE.

As I made clear in Chapter 3, the first word of the steps—*We*—turned me off, but in some subtle way it also attracted me. I had always been a loner, and when people hit me with the slogan "*I* can't, but *we* can," I gagged. But the fact that the steps were in the past tense and the word *we* referred to the first hundred people who got sober in AA made it a little bit more palatable.

My resistance to being a *we* evaporated when I began to understand the Buddhist concept of *anatta*, not-self. Up to that point, I had realized that "terminal uniqueness" would get me drunk and that, as my AA sponsor grumbled to me with great frequency, I'd better learn "to identify, not compare." I sat in AA meetings, listening to people tell their stories, and increasingly the detail of events blurred and I saw the commonalities in the physical and emotional progression of the disease we shared. When people spoke of their anger, grief, or shame, I knew exactly how they felt. They were telling my heart story.

It was remarkably clear to me that we all want to be happy, but trapped in ignorance and addiction, we keep doing things that might give us a moment of relief but always eventually lead to pain. One day I watched my dog gulp down an unguarded bowl of guacamole, then throw up. I identified with *her*. She and guacamole were not different from me and martinis. I became increasingly aware that almost all species "look for love in all the wrong places" and end up suffering as the result. I finally was able to see that all sentient beings are made up of aggregates, as I am, and that we're all in motion all the time.

When I first came to AA, I also fought the notion that I, the Control Queen of Greenwich Village, was powerless over *anything*, and I insistently denied that my life was unmanageable—until the day I described earlier when my AA sponsor asked me, "Do you really think a person whose life is manageable would attempt suicide as many times as you have?" My understanding of *powerless* and *unmanageable* became much more consequential when I looked at my drinking in terms of dependent origination and the law of karma.

As I described at the beginning of Chapter 10, because I am an alcoholic, the law of dependent origination asserts that when I have *contact* with alcohol, then *feeling*, *craving*, and *clinging* ensure that I will drink to drunkenness. I have absolutely no choice after I take the first drink. I am powerless. When I pick up a drink, biologically and psychologically I am "programmed" to drink continuously and repeatedly.

When I was an alcoholic who was not in recovery, my life was unmanageable because my mind was unmanageable. The subtext of my intentions always involved drinking—to cover up something I had done or said while drinking, or to put myself into situations where I could drink again as soon as possible. Those intentions became the actions and words—the karma—of my daily life. The need to drink took a huge amount of energy and made getting through each day very difficult: I had to get up and go to work when I was throwing up from the night before, I had to get through long days of demanding work with horrendous hangovers, and I had to act as if I still had dignity in the face of all the humiliations that an alcoholic incurs.

When I deeply grasped the underlying effects of dependent origination and karma on my alcoholism, I understood power-lessness and unmanageability with an intensity I had not previ-ously imagined. The comforting aspect of this understanding is the absolute lawfulness of dependent origination and karma. If I don't drink, I won't get drunk and I won't screw up my life.

STEP TWO: CAME TO BELIEVE THAT A POWER GREATER THAN OURSELVES COULD RESTORE US TO SANITY.

Within the context of AA, using a Group of Drunks as my Higher Power and expressing gratitude to Honey Pie worked and contin-ues to work for me. When I listen with an open heart and mind to others in recovery, my faith in restoration to sanity is absolute—as long as I don't pick up a drink.

When I began to delve into Buddhism again in my forties, I had a nagging concern that my agnosticism, at least in relation-ship to conventional religions, would be a problem. The Buddha himself relieved that apprehension in his teachings. He made it clear that he was a human being, not a god. He did not teach that there was a God. He did not teach that there was not a God. Whenever he was questioned about the existence of a Creator God, he refused to answer and insisted that metaphysical ques-tions such as this one were irrelevant to what he taught: suffer-ing and the end of suffering.

What is clear in all the Buddha's teachings is that there is one great power we must cultivate if we are to end *dukkha*: that power is mindfulness. Mindfulness is awareness in the present moment of our thoughts, words, and actions—right down to the inhalation and exhalation of breath. Development of mindfulness, which we'll look at more closely in the next chapter, is not an easy task. In the Buddha's time, training the mind was frequently compared to taming a wild elephant—a task that is painstaking but absolutely necessary if the elephant (or mind) is to be of any real use.

I came to believe that mindfulness could restore me to sanity because, if I were mindful, I would no longer make decisions based in greed, hatred, and delusion. Rather, mindfulness can lead me to insight, to seeing things as they really are, and I can consequently think, act, and speak skillfully—harming no one, including myself. With mindfulness, I can create for myself karma that is sane and beneficial to myself and others. I can realistically anticipate consequences and act accordingly.

STEP THREE: MADE A DECISION TO TURN OUR WILL AND OUR LIVES OVER TO THE CARE OF GOD *as we understood [god]*.

Relatively early in sobriety, I was able to make the decision to turn my will and my life over to the *care* of a Group of Drunks because I had absolute faith, based on observation of others' recovery, that the people in AA wanted only sobriety for me and that "The AA Program Works If You Work It." Making the decision to turn my will and my life over to the care of Buddhist practices and teachings actually took me quite a bit longer because understanding them required not only faith but also study, patient reflection, and meditation practice.

I immediately understood the concept that I could live a life of nonharming, but it took me a long time to grasp *dukkha*, impermanence, karma, and not-self and what their implications are for everyday life. I had had to understand at least the basic teachings before I knew that I really wanted to live according to the Dharma and was able to make the decision to do so.

The third step was one that I had to take repeatedly, because I would turn over my life and will—and then take them back, on an almost daily basis, sometimes on an hourly one. I think I would have been sucked into remorse over my wishy-washiness had it not been for a passage in Chapter 5 of *Alcoholics Anonymous* read at many meetings:

> No one among us has been able to maintain anything like perfect adherence to these principles [Twelve Steps]. We are not saints. The point is that we are willing to grow along spiritual lines. The principles we have set down are guides to progress. We claim spiritual progress rather than spiritual perfection. (p. 60)

When I had problems living a householder's life according to the Dharma, I learned to gently remind myself that I was seeking spiritual progress rather than perfection. In this way I increasingly assimilated the teachings and became more and more mindful. After several years, I became aware that I really *wanted* to live according to the Buddha's teachings and that somewhere along the way, without consciously planning to, I had already made the decision to try to live a life of nonharming.

In the third-step prayer (*Alcoholics Anonymous*, p. 63), one sentence begins, "Relieve me of the bondage of self" [so that I can do God's will]. In Buddhism, we can be relieved of the bondage of self only when we begin to understand *anatta*, not-self, as described in Chapter 7. With this understanding, we can truly "do unto others as we would have them do unto us" because we know that they *are* us. There is no absolute separation. Whatever we do to help them helps us. And it's easier to live a life of nonharming when we know that whatever we do to others, we are doing to ourselves.

STEP FOUR: MADE A SEARCHING AND FEARLESS MORAL INVENTORY OF OURSELVES.

STEP FIVE: ADMITTED TO GOD, TO OURSELVES, AND TO ANOTHER HUMAN BEING THE EXACT NATURE OF OUR WRONGS.

After I began to practice Buddhism as a way of life, the fourth and fifth steps for me meant developing insight so I could see things as they really are. The Buddhist teacher Jack Kornfield once commented, "Self-discovery is never good news." It hadn't been for me when I did AA's fourth step—or when I began to seek insight into my intentions, thoughts, actions, and words.

Understanding the relationship between intentions and actions and becoming uncomfortably aware of how untamed my mind was motivated me to want to bring my mind under usable control so I could live a life of mindfulness. As my awareness grew as the result of meditation practice, I could see the changes beginning to happen in my life. I could see the progress, if not the perfection, and I realized that—because of my own impermanence—I was undertaking a pursuit that would last for my whole lifetime because I was making my own karma.

Increasingly, I discovered, when I shared my experiences with the Group of Drunks at a meeting, I could see and articulate the patterns of my thoughts, words, and actions with greater and greater clarity. Because of the factor of insight, I hid—and repressed—no secrets. I admitted them all to myself and these other human beings.

STEP SIX: WERE ENTIRELY READY TO HAVE GOD REMOVE ALL THESE DEFECTS OF CHARACTER.

STEP SEVEN: HUMBLY ASKED [THE HIGHER POWER] TO REMOVE OUR SHORTCOMINGS.

I had always been uncomfortable with the words *moral inventory* and *wrongs* in Steps Four and Five and *defects of character* and *shortcomings* in Steps Six and Seven because they are so judgmental. Yes, I acknowledged that I had hurt people and myself. But within the concepts of Buddhism, I could see that I had created a lot of "bad" karma as the result of a disease and that my actions toward myself and others had been very unskillful, causing harm. This understanding motivated me to want to be truly, mindfully present in my life so that I would create, instead, "good" karma, actions that harmed no one, including me.

The possibility that I could live a skillful life depended upon two things: my staying sober and my learning to be mindful. I embraced sobriety by going to AA meetings. When I shared problems I was having, I was asking the Group of Drunks to help me. My trust in the AA program became so strong that I was ready—and willing—to have AA members "take away" my problems through the wisdom of their experience, strength, and hope and my own certainty that there was no separation between me and them. I could trust them.

I learned to develop mindfulness through intentional practice. Just as I needed to go to AA meetings to interact with my Group of Drunks, so too did I need to spend time with a sangha, a group of people with whom I could meditate and study the Dharma, and I had to commit myself to a daily sitting practice, just as in the beginning of my sobriety I went to meetings every day. (I'll expand on developing mindfulness in the next chapter.)

It became clear to me that for my personal spiritual journey, I need both AA and the Dharma. AA alone does not fulfill all my spiritual needs, and Buddhism alone will not keep me sober.

STEP EIGHT: MADE A LIST OF ALL
PERSONS WE HAD HARMED, AND
BECAME WILLING TO MAKE AMENDS
TO THEM ALL.

STEP NINE: MADE DIRECT AMENDS TO SUCH PEOPLE WHEREVER POSSIBLE, EXCEPT WHEN TO DO SO WOULD INJURE THEM OR OTHERS.

By the time I became engaged by the Buddha's teachings, I had already made direct amends to the people I had harmed "wherever possible." Even so, my name sat there at the top of the list. I had made wonderful amends to myself simply by getting sober. I had begun to eat, sleep, and exercise in healthy ways. But I still felt myself spiritually bearing an enormous karmic burden from my drinking years.

Understanding that I could not change my past karma, I determined that genuine amends to myself were possible only through my making a commitment to trying to live according to the Dharma. If I did so, I would know spiritual transformation that would make me "happy, joyous, and free" (an AA phrase). Peace would begin with me and would spread in a ripple effect to those whose lives I touched. There was no better way to make amends, and I became a resolute practitioner of Insight Meditation as a way of working Steps Nine and Ten.

STEP TEN: CONTINUED TO TAKE PERSONAL INVENTORY AND WHEN WE WERE WRONG PROMPTLY ADMITTED IT.

Every time I sit down to meditate, I am taking personal inventory. Dipa Ma, an Indian meditation teacher, gave the advice "If you want to know the nature of mind, sit down and watch it." Ajahn Chah, a Burmese meditation teacher, suggested that we sit down "in the middle of the room" and throw open the doors and windows (of our mind) to see who comes in. When we sit in meditation, we re-create, in our minds, a microcosm of our world. When we are attentive to what comes up in our minds, we will find a parade of desire, aversion, restlessness, sleepiness, and doubt (the Five Hindrances, discussed in Chapter 12), changing costumes from time to time, then arising and passing away again.

As new meditators, we may find this "monkey mind," swinging from branch to branch, surprising and perhaps even alarming. But with experience, we can see the insubstantiality of our thoughts and become increasingly aware in our daily lives that we don't have to act on a thought just because it comes up. We learn this lesson early in AA: just because we think of drinking or want to drink doesn't mean we have to. The same concept applies across the board: Just because we want to blow our horn at the pokey driver in front of us, doesn't mean we have to. Just because we are so attracted to someone that we'd like to have an extramarital affair, doesn't mean we have to. Just because we think we can get away with cheating on our income taxes, doesn't mean we have to. The trick with unskillful thoughts is to be present in the moment and to acknowledge the insubstantiality of these thoughts and feelings, then to let them go without acting on them.

An inventory sees what's on the shelf—too much or too little —and we are so distracted in our daily lives that it's hard to take personal inventory. When we sit down to meditate, the inventory—

welcome or unwelcome—comes to us. With insight, we can see whether our inventory is "in balance" or not.

STEP ELEVEN: SOUGHT THROUGH
PRAYER AND MEDITATION TO IMPROVE
OUR CONSCIOUS CONTACT WITH GOD
as we understood [god], PRAYING ONLY
FOR KNOWLEDGE OF [GOD'S] WILL
FOR US AND THE POWER TO CARRY
THAT OUT.

As I noted in Chapter 3, Group *of Drunks* was the acronym I used for *God,* and I called my Higher Power Honey Pie. Within AA I had understood *prayer* to mean speaking and *meditation* to mean listening (at meetings). After I became a committed Buddhist practitioner, my understanding of this step expanded greatly.

My concept of prayer essentially became the wish and the intention to live more mindfully a life of nonharming. This kind of "prayer" was not directed to anyone except myself. Just as in the beginning of sobriety I made a commitment each morning to staying sober, I now added the intention to try to be truly present, in my sobriety, for each moment of that day. My effort to keep this intention strengthened as my understanding of the teachings of the Buddha deepened. In AA it was enough to understand that I had to stay sober because I am an alcoholic. Now I understood that I had to be sober to be present for my life. The more I realized the peace and joy of being present, the more highly motivated I was to stay sober *and* to cultivate mindfulness.

Meditation for me became "listening" not just to the Group of Drunks but also to all the beings I came into contact with—human or otherwise—and to myself. An important part of "improving" this "conscious contact" was to listen, or to try to directly experience, each contact in the moment and without old stories, without projections into the past or the future. The only way I could improve the contact was through insight, seeing things as they are, and the power to do so was practiced, cultivated, and nourished by my formal meditation practice.

STEP TWELVE: HAVING HAD A SPIRITUAL AWAKENING AS THE RESULT OF THESE STEPS, WE TRIED TO CARRY THIS MESSAGE TO ALCOHOLICS, AND TO PRACTICE THESE PRINCIPLES IN ALL OUR AFFAIRS.

My spiritual awakening has been quite slow. I sometimes have had the irreverent thought that if I had been awakened by the kind of spiritual hot flash that Bill W., the cofounder of AA, had or that the Buddha had the night of his awakening, I probably would have had a heart attack and died. No, for me the experience has been much slower, step by step, one day at a time. I have kept in mind that detested AA slogan *Anything Worth Doing Is Worth Doing Slowly*. I have had no choice but to exercise patience and consistent effort—knowing I was aiming for progress not perfection.

I was inspired to not give up on this step by the idea often expressed at AA meetings that in our daily lives, we interact with many people who have never had contact with AA or read the Big Book (*Alcoholics Anonymous*). In a sense my behavior may be the only Big Book that such people ever "read." This idea is true inside AA as well as outside: Knowing that other alcoholics—not just struggling drunks but also struggling sober people—would be affected by how I worked the steps and how I lived as a sober person helped me to stay sober. It wasn't the kind of ego trip that some celebrities have gone on, breaking their anonymity "to help others," then getting drunk or being such blowhards that people would comment, "If this is what AA sobriety is like, you can have it." Rather, to help *themselves* stay sober, people in AA meetings make themselves vulnerable by sharing terribly difficult life situations and asking for (spiritual) help.

These people have been my models. These people have been my Big Book. I wanted to be like them. I wanted to be the kind of person that other people would want to be—not so that I could be an "AA star" but so that I could live happily. One day I asked the most serene, happy person I had met in AA how she did it. She replied, "Have you ever watched a swan gliding across a pond? Well, if you could look under the water, you'd see that the swan is paddling like hell. That's how you do it. You really put that kind of effort into working the steps."

At some point I realized that, as a Buddhist practitioner, I might be the only Dharma the people I meet ever see/read/hear. I believe passionately that the world would be a better place if everyone embraced nonharming. But I am well aware of a comment a woman made at a meditation retreat: "My parents hate me when I'm a Buddhist but love me when I'm a *buddha*." The point is not to go around preaching the Dharma but rather to realize that when we just live our lives, *nothing is ever lost*. Most of us have no idea what effect we have on other beings and even the environment around us. But we are making a difference—whether we intend to or not.

The most dramatic illustration I know of this "when-a-butterfly-moves-its-wings-in-China-the-weather-in-Nova-Scotia-changes" effect is the story of King Ashoka. In the third century BCE, he ruled much of the land that now makes up India, and he increased the size of his kingdom through ruthless, brutal conquest. One morning after a particularly bloody battle, he walked across the battlefield, trying to step over the grisly remains of soldiers—his own men and the enemy's—strewn everywhere. Momentarily, he really *got it* that he had caused the carnage surrounding him. Just then he saw one figure moving on the field—a Buddhist monk slowly walking among the bodies. The calmness of the monk's demeanor moved Ashoka deeply, and he approached him and asked how he could be so serene. The monk replied that he followed the teachings of the Buddha, and Ashoka implored the monk to share with him these teachings.

Ashoka became such an avid and committed student that he changed the philosophical stance of his kingdom from war to peace. He created hospitals and even veterinary clinics. He saw that his people were fed and cared for. His children carried the Dharma to countries throughout Southeast Asia; from there and India, the Buddha's teachings eventually spread worldwide. Several millennia later, a visitor to northern India can still find archaeological ruins of "Ashoka's pillars"—stelae with carved teachings from the Dharma—throughout what had been Ashoka's kingdom. If that monk had not walked calmly across that battlefield, I would not have written this book and you would not be reading it.

Knowing that nothing is ever lost inspires me to mindfully "practice these principles"—the Twelve Steps and the Dharma— "in all my affairs."

12

THE EIGHTFOLD SOBER PATH

As I've mentioned above, the Twelve Steps describe what the first hundred sober members of Alcoholics Anonymous did to become and stay sober—in other words, the steps demonstrate how people who get sober act. The Eightfold Path exemplifies what an enlightened being, the Buddha, has done to become enlightened and how he behaves; as such it is template for anyone wishing to become an enlightened being. I'd like to revisit the Eightfold Path discussed in Chapter 9 and see how the wisdom teachings (wise understanding and thought), the morality teachings (wise speech, action, and livelihood), and the mental discipline teachings (wise effort, mindfulness, and concentration) play out in terms of sobriety.

SOBER UNDERSTANDING

Within the Dharma, the term *wise understanding* means grasping the Four Noble Truths, impermanence, dependent origination, karma, and not-self. In AA, *wise understanding*, in the salty expression of my Greenwich Village home group, means "You don't drink if your ass falls off. If it falls off, you take it to an AA meeting and find a new way to sit." The corollary is "There's no situation so bad that a drink won't make it worse."

When I meld the Dharma and AA, I attain *sober understanding*. The basic concepts of the two ways of living fit together so comfortably that for me, they are inseparable.

With sober understanding, if I consider the Four Noble Truths and substitute the word *addiction* or *alcoholism* for *dukkha*, I get an accurate picture of my life as an active alcoholic. In the First Noble Truth, the Buddha said that *dukkha* was pervasive in our daily lives. My disease, my *dukkha*, sometimes in small, sometimes in large ways, was certainly present in all aspects of my life. Like the Buddha's Second Noble Truth, my *dukkha*'s origin—whether genetic or social or a combination of the two—lay in unrelenting craving: the insatiable thirst for alcohol that underlies the disease of alcoholism. The Buddha, in the Third Noble Truth, said that cessation of *dukkha* was possible only through the "remainderless extinction" of that craving. Without doubt, the only way I could achieve relief from the *dukkha* of my disease was by following a path of Truth analogous to the Eightfold Path—using the Twelve Steps as the roadmap for recovery—and going to AA meetings and not drinking. Only this could be the "remainderless extinction" of my disease.

Wise understanding of dependent origination and impermanence enabled me to finally, truly achieve sober understanding that the happiness I thought drinking would bring me could not last unchanged. There might be a short time after the first drink or two when I might have fun, but—through the phases of dependent origination that made me powerless over alcohol—I would continue to drink well past the fun part. I came to see clearly that as long as I continued to drink alcohol, my karma would always be to end up with me saying and doing things that caused me and others embarrassment and pain. *Dukkha*.

An important factor in my accepting the fact that I must not drink came with my comprehension of *anatta*, of not-self, even though initially I didn't use that term. As long as I thought of myself as being unique, separate, something special, I had nagging whispers in my head that said things like "But *you're* different," "*You* can beat this thing," and "Show some grit, girl!" What a relief it was to know that this disease *wasn't* personal, that lack of willpower *wasn't* my problem, and that I was an ordinary, garden-variety drunk. I gained the deep, sober understanding that I was not different from—was not separate from—royalty or inmates or anyone else with whom I share this disease.

No matter how much I had rationalized and lied about my drinking to others and to myself, sober understanding cut through any possible delusion I may have had that I could ever safely drink again.

SOBER THOUGHT /
SOBER INTENTION

As so often happened, one day in early sobriety I went to an AA meeting where the topic was exactly what I needed at that moment—in this case, not holding on to resentments. During the discussion, one man commented, "For me, hanging on to a resentment against someone is like saying, 'I'll show you! I'll kill *me*.'" That observation got my attention, though I didn't completely comprehend it . . . yet. Other people made remarks such as "When I hold on to a resentment against someone, they're fine but I've got acid in *my* stomach," and "I just don't want someone I resent living rent-free in my head."

Although I was nodding in agreement with all these comments, I still found myself wondering how to get rid of resentments. Someone suggested that the way to get over a resentment toward someone was to pray for that person. In my early sobriety, that strategy didn't work at all: I found myself telling Honey Pie all kinds of awful things that should happen to my personal villain du jour. I had enough clarity to see that I needed to get rid of my resentments, but I didn't have enough wisdom to know how.

When I began to work with the Buddha's wisdom teachings, I came to understand that wise thought/intention/aspiration meant renouncing all thoughts of harming and all ill-will against all others, and ourselves. Because we shape our world with our minds, all thoughts or intentions of animosity plant the seeds for harming through our words or actions at some point in the future.

For this reason, my Buddhist commitment to nonharming made it obligatory that I renounce all thoughts of harming that arose in my mind. As a recovering alcoholic, sober thought made it equally obvious that I could not indulge animosity and resentments and stay sober because, to use one of the AA slogans, *I Can't But We Can.* Every time I found myself clinging to a resentment, I was separating myself from others, creating a sense of self—an I—and negating my basic understanding of how critical it is to recovery to be a "we." It didn't matter whether the object of my hostility was another person in recovery or not. The dynamics of separation through enmity and blame were the same: I would be taken out of the present moment and thrust into a story of my own making to justify the ill feelings. This situation violated "wise thought" and blatantly showed that sober thought was not present.

SOBER SPEECH

While I was drinking, my mouth seemed to have a life of its own and my speech would have fit a checklist of what the Buddha said should be avoided in order to practice wise speech. I lied, I was verbally abusive, and I indulged in frivolous speech such as gossip. An informal definition used by many AA members is that an alcoholic is an egomaniac with an inferiority complex—a description that fit me quite well when I was drinking and followed me into recovery.

This characteristic personality combination energized my drunk speech, especially when I violated all three aspects of wise speech by building myself up at another's expense. I could make myself look very good by misrepresenting myself and others; I could make others cringe by my abusive verbal attacks, and I used gossip to spread disunity by talking about others in a negative way, perhaps "for their own good," by inflating their bad qualities, sometimes through outright lies.

In sobriety, I had to deal first with lying to myself. I had to acknowledge my alcoholism to myself and then to others before my recovery could begin. Recovery is literally a matter of life and death; neither abusive nor frivolous speech is appropriate or helpful in any way to oneself or to others. Sober speech is mindful speech—embodying both truth and usefulness and expressed in a way and at a time that it can be heard.

This last point necessarily involves whether to speak, as well as when and how. In many instances, wise speech/sober speech requires no speech at all. When our words would be untrue or frivolous or harmful, we are better to not speak. And when someone else needs to speak, we can show our greatest respect for sober speech by listening, by not interrupting, by not being so caught up in what our rejoinder will be that we don't hear the other person.

Sober speech is thus a form of spiritual generosity. We must, in the words of AA's Preamble, share our experience, strength, and hope, that we may solve our common problem and help others to recover from alcoholism. This type of sober speech can include sharing our experiences at meetings, talking with newcomers, making or accepting telephone calls from an "alcoholic who still suffers" (sober or not), and listening to others with mindful and loving attention. With sober speech, we do not verbally attack others, to their faces or behind their backs. With sober understanding and sober intention, we can use our speech as a way to strengthen our interconnectedness with all others, promoting the healing grace of recovery.

SOBER ACTION

When I was drinking, I acted upon any idea that came into my head, and some, it seemed, that never made that transit between my ears. In sobriety, I learned to distinguish between actions that lead toward a drink and actions that lead away from a drink. I also learned to avoid Them. *Them* was usually defined as "people, places, and things that I associated with drinking enough that they could make me vulnerable." This guideline, combined with the Dharma definition of *wise action* as refraining from anything that would cause harm to oneself or others, came to be my working principle of *sober action*.

I especially embraced sober action within the context of the Five Precepts, which we first looked at in Chapter 9, because my sobriety depended upon specifically changing my attitudes and actions in relationship to those areas of behavior.

Sober Action and the Five Precepts

1. *Avoid harming or killing other beings.* When I drank, it was as if I had a wall around me that insulated me from really connecting with others. I didn't know that the wall was glass and that people who cared enough about me to look could see through it. I didn't know that the glass, rather than keeping others out, was imprisoning me inside. The glass was not half empty or half full; it was *completely* filled with the alcohol and drugs that were inside me. I cared so little for others and was so unaware of them that I didn't even notice when I was harming them. And in my alcoholic denial, I certainly was not aware of how much I was harming myself.

My first sober action had to be renouncing everything—people, places, things, even ideas—that could in any way harm me by leading me to a drink. Only when I learned from sober friends how to love myself could I begin to sincerely care about others. Only when I learned from the Dharma that I *am* the "others" could I make a commitment, as long as I did not pick up a drink, with my whole heart and mind, to nonharming.

2. *Avoid taking what is not freely given.* In my alcoholic self-centeredness, I had a grand sense of entitlement. Whether something was given or not mattered little to me. I took what I wanted, when I wanted it. I didn't literally steal things from people or shoplift, but in a way this was only because it never occurred to me. What I took were love, ideas, power. Climbing the career ladder, I went for what I wanted and took it. Nothing stood in my way. Although I paid lip service to environmental and social causes, much of my motivation was posturing and acting out my image of myself. If the causes I cared about had ever demanded sacrifice beyond periodically not eating domestic grapes or buying from a particular store, I would have been incapable of taking action. I was a taker, not a giver.

When I got sober, one of the slogans hammered home was "We keep it [sobriety] by giving it away." The giving away was done through "service"—holding office in AA groups, making coffee for meetings, sponsoring newcomers, doing whatever needed doing with the understanding that doing so would help us stay sober. A lovely expression of this willingness to give was stated in the "responsibility pledge" that had emerged as the keynote of AA's thirtieth anniversary convention in Toronto in 1965:

I am responsible.
Whenever anyone, anywhere, reaches out for help,
I want the hand of AA to always be there.
And for that: I am responsible.

In becoming sober action, this principle for me morphed into not only giving freely whenever anyone reached out, but also giving freely—whether someone reached out or not—those actions or words that could bring compassion, unity, and helpfulness to those who needed it. I learned the sober truth that generosity resides in the heart, not the purse.

3. *Avoid sexual misconduct.* As an active alcoholic I was a slut. In a blackout I could end up in bed with almost anyone, but even when I wasn't drunk I used sexual behavior and seduction as a way to build my ego up at someone else's expense. Conquest was fodder for my self-esteem even as shame eroded it. When I got sober, I had enough sense to know that sexual misconduct with someone in AA could be life-threatening to them or to me. But outside of AA, I was more selective than I had been while drinking, but my behavior was the same ego trip. Only when I began to work within the Dharma with the concept of harming people through sexual activity did I come to see the karmic consequences of sexual misconduct to myself, to my partner's family, to the fabric of community. Sober action here took the form of distinguishing between need for affection and lust for ego-gratification and acting with kindness and affection to establish bonds of intimacy and giving the kind of unselfish attention that sustains true loving.

4. *Avoid harmful speech.* As I noted above, for me this sober precept became to refrain from untrue, frivolous, abusive, and

ill-timed speech and instead to see to it that my words did not add a drop of pain to what is already a world too full of suffering.

5. *Avoid intoxicants that dull the mind.* Early in sobriety I could understand why I shouldn't take the first drink, but I didn't understand why other "recreational drugs" weren't acceptable in AA. Later, in Buddhism, I learned about spiritual practice as a way of developing insight, which is defined as seeing things as they really are. It became absolutely obvious to me that if I really want clarity of mind, why would I ingest a substance that clouds the mind? Although a cold beer on a hot day or a fine wine in a good restaurant may momentarily look good to me, sober action for me would be to abstain from mind-altering substances even if I were not an alcoholic.

Many Dharma teachers have noted that violating the fifth precept undermines our ability to live by the other four. For me as an alcoholic, *undermines* is an inadequate word for what happens. If I drink, I *do* harm others, I *do* take what is not freely given, I *do* engage in sexual misconduct, and I *do* cause suffering by my words. If I drink, all the Dharma precepts for living a life of nonharming go down the toilet.

SOBER LIVELIHOOD

Sometimes at the beginning of Buddhist meditation retreats longer than a week, the teachers ask several questions. They may include "How many of you have practiced meditation longer than five years?" and "How many of you work in so-called helping professions?" Longer retreats tend to attract people who have been meditating for a long time, and when this combination occurs, a remarkably high percentage indicate that they work in helping professions.

There is a curious parallel in recovery. With the exception of people in a few professions such as law, teaching, and the arts, most of the people I know who have been sober five or ten years have changed professions from what they did while they were drinking and now earn their living by working in a helping profession. In my immediate circle, one law clerk to a judge is now a therapist, one stockbroker became a physician's assistant, and many other friends have become social workers.

This correspondence is not really surprising. With long-term Dharma study, we increasingly understand at a level that sometimes feels cellular that we are interconnected with all beings, that harming them harms ourselves, that helping them helps ourselves. It only seems natural that we want to spend our time in compassionate work that eases suffering and helps others. In AA, one of the recognized bases for strengthening and maintaining our recovery is through "service," to other alcoholics, to our group, and to AA as a whole. We carry the habits we develop in AA into our everyday world beyond AA, including our work. In the words of Step Twelve, we "practice these principles in all our affairs." There seems to be a natural progression during recovery of wanting consistency in the quality of our lives, whether in or outside of AA rooms, that leads us to find a way to "practice these principles" in our work or to change our work. Sober livelihood is discovering how we can be the same wise and compassionate person in our work life as well as when we are in an AA meeting.

SOBER EFFORT

Just as the Buddha emphasized the necessity of using wise effort as an underlying factor for practicing the other seven parts of the Eightfold Path, so too throughout the Twelve Steps the urgency of bringing willingness to our program is stressed. The terms *effort* and *willingness* share connotations across the programs. Both imply an intention: in Buddhism, to cultivate mental discipline and nonharming; in AA, to recover by working the steps. In both practices, to fulfill this intention, we must be willing to make the effort to do so.

Because the Eightfold Path and the Twelve Steps are not *rules* but instead reflect the actions and behavior of successful adherents who have gone before, both reflect the AA slogan *If You Want What We Have, You'll Do What We Do*. When conjoined, the two pieces give us the motivation for sober effort through our deep understanding of both the intention and the outcome that comprise them. We make the sober effort to cultivate sobriety by consistently practicing the Twelve Steps, just as we make the sober effort to cultivate insight through a consistent mindfulness mediation practice.

SOBER MINDFULNESS

The first lesson in mindfulness that we are given in AA usually is "Always ask yourself whether what you're about to do will lead you toward or away from a drink." There is also an emphasis on living sober in the present moment, rather than wallowing in the past or projecting with fear or grandiosity into the future. The

Dharma teaches us to stay in the moment because it is the only reality and our actions in the present—skillful or unskillful—determine our future karma.

Sober mindfulness is staying in the present moment, understanding that loss of mindful attention can pave the road to the kinds of unskillful actions that can lead us to drinking again. Cultivating mindfulness in many ways is the most critical aspect of both working the Dharma and working the steps. Its importance cannot be overemphasized. In Chapter 11, I described how mindfulness is my Dharmic Higher Power. *Sober mindfulness is my single greatest protection against ever picking up a drink again.*

SOBER CONCENTRATION

The discussion of wise concentration in Chapter 11 stressed two points: we develop concentration skills through practice, just as a musician develops musical skills through practice, and the hindrances that arise during meditation are the same ones that occur in daily life, often so subtly that we do not recognize their presence. Sober concentration recognizes that just as these hindrances can break down our concentration, so too can they shatter our sobriety. Let's look at the hindrances again, in terms of sobriety.

The Five Hindrances to Sober Concentration

1. *Desire.* For alcoholics, desire is usually the craving for a mood-altering substance, sometimes specifically for alcohol or a drug, but sometimes we may experience a kind of generalized yen for something that is missing. In AA, we very often hear or see the acronym *HALT*—"Don't get too Hungry, Angry, Lonely, or

Tired." When any one or more of these conditions occurs, our wires seem to be crossed so that we interpret it as an urge to drink. The very important lesson we learn in sobriety is that just because we want to drink doesn't mean that we have to.

In the joining of AA and the Dharma, we can transfer this lesson to the Five Precepts, knowing that just because we may strongly want to take something not freely given or gossip or have an extramarital affair, doesn't mean we have to. We can see desire for what it is: desire.

2. *Aversion.* As active alcoholics, we may react to almost anything in our lives with aversion—that something is not good or good enough or even enough. Many of us are also aversive to emotional pain and have numbed ourselves with alcohol to avoid it. Such aversive reactions follow most of us into sobriety and may cause us to harbor dislike or resentment for years. As our understanding of the Dharma deepens, we begin to see that a great deal of our aversive reactions are the mechanisms by which we create a sense of the almighty self. Anytime we feel dislike for or we're angry with or we blame someone, we are driving a wedge of separation between ourselves and others. When we have insight of the Dharma, we can see aversion as simply aversion and not break the interconnection that we have with all beings. This does not mean that we have to like all events and beings, but when we can label aversion as aversion, we do not have to react with old, unskillful means.

3. *Restlessness.* In early sobriety, many of us experience extremes of physical restlessness as a result of withdrawal from chemical dependency. Much mental restlessness—especially in the form of short attention span—may also be the result of physical withdrawal and its frequent attendant, anxiety. When restlessness is so strong

that it shatters our sitting meditation, we can instead do walking meditation or a practice such as *metta* (discussed in Chapter 14). Again, the important thing is to recognize the restlessness for what it is, without making up stories about the feelings.

4. *Sloth and torpor.* As with all the hindrances, the most important step is to recognize them. When sleepiness sets in, we need to ask first if there is a legitimate reason for it—such as being very tired, the *T* in *HALT*. If so, a rest is in order. The Dharma suggestions for dealing with this condition range from standing up, taking a fast walk, looking at a bright light, to raising the energy level by intensely investigating just what sleepiness feels like. When we have experience with AA and the Dharma, we can more quickly identify the need for rest versus the need for greater attention.

5. *Doubt.* The Buddha said that doubt is the most challenging of the hindrances because it is self-generated and therefore seems so rational. In recovery, doubt's analog is denial, one of the most prevalent characteristics of addiction. We have a disease that tells us we do not have a disease, that we go to the wrong meetings or have the wrong sponsor, that maybe AA works for others but won't work for us. In Buddhist practice, when we recognize doubt, it often dissipates under scrutiny, but if it isn't put to rest, it is very helpful to talk with a teacher or spiritual friend. In AA, we can talk to our sponsor, who usually will shoot down denial/doubt quite quickly.

Sober concentration enables us to learn, through meditative practice, to recognize the hindrances for what they are, whether they arise when we're sitting on a cushion, on a chair at an AA meeting, or in a booth in a restaurant. As we become more skillful in recognizing them, we become increasingly skillful in responding rather than reacting. (*Re-acting* literally is acting again in old ways—that is, perpetuating ancient, twisted karma.)

Sober concentration also strengthens our ability to recognize our "primary purpose" ("to stay sober and help other alcoholics achieve sobriety"—as stated in the AA Preamble) and to avoid the "selfing"—the deluded attempt at creation of a separate, permanent, unique self that in fact does not and cannot exist—that can distract us from that purpose.

13

THE DHARMA-
PROMISES

JUST AS I LOOKED at the Dharma through the eyes of recovery when I became involved in Buddhism, so too did I begin to see
the AA program illuminated by Buddhist teachings. Looking
back, I can perceive that I first integrated these two programs/
teachings as I strove to live a sober life according to the Twelve
Steps. The steps are the template for my life on a daily basis, and
I first was able to consciously identify the impact that the Dharma
was having on my AA program when I reflected on the steps. As
my relationship with the Dharma deepened—but never at the
expense or displacement of the AA program—I realized that I was

practicing both AA and Dharma principles "in all my affairs" and that the promises on pages 83 and 84 of the book *Alcoholics Anonymous* (4th edition) were taking on new meaning for me.

During the first decade or so of my sobriety I was in awe of the tender unfolding of those promises in my life. The changes happened so gradually that only with hindsight could I recognize that each one was coming true for me. As I described in Chapter 4, about the time I thought I "had gotten" everything promised and was ready for a certificate of accomplishment, the external things I treasured in my life fell away and I felt as if I were at ground zero again, starting over. The faith that carried me through my early days of sobriety had proven to me that I could get through anything, and this "informed faith" sustained me as I began to rebuild my life. Again.

This time, however, the Dharma was working in concert with AA's promises, and they became more meaningful than I could ever have imagined. With this melding of the Dharma and AA's promises now in my life, I felt as if I had previously been looking at a tapestry from the wrong side—a tangle of multicolored threads—but now had turned it over so I could see the patterns that its beautiful colors were creating. Although I had tried to work the AA Steps in sequence, the hologramlike nature of Buddhism meant that I was working with all of AA's promises simultaneously, though I only was able to understand them in this new way one at a time. So let me take up these fresh insights in the same order as the promises that appear in *Alcoholics Anonymous* on pages 83 and 84.

We are going to know a new freedom and a new happiness.

My initial understanding of this statement essentially embraced freedom from the control of addiction and happiness based on being grateful for what I have. In studying the Dharma, I found that the two concepts of freedom and happiness are inextricably linked in a profound way that is basic to all the teachings of the Buddha. Put very simply: happiness (or the end of suffering, nirvana) is the "extinction of thirst" (the freedom that comes from the end of clinging, grasping, and attachment to all that is impermanent, which is everything). This concept takes my earlier discovery that I could have a happy sobriety by extinguishing the irresistible thirst for alcohol, then extends and generalizes it to all aspects of my life.

All beings want to be happy, to be free from suffering. But we human beings, who are impermanent, fairly consistently try to gain happiness by getting and holding on to that which is also impermanent. When I came to terms with my alcoholism, I had enough sense to realize that I would be miserable as long as I clung to chemical mood-changers. The happy glow that I passed through in each drinking episode was always short-lived and became just plain shorter over the years.

Greed (my desire for alcohol), aversion (denial that alcohol was the source of my problems), and delusion (that I could drink safely) had been rampant while I was still drinking. So I stopped drinking, but I still believed that I would find happiness in the right job (until I got fired), the right relationship (until I got dumped), the right car (until a deer jumped off a hillside onto the hood and wrecked it), the right house (until an earthquake cracked the foundation), the right pet (until she died), and on and on and on.

I had indeed gotten most of the objects of desire I thought would bring me happiness, but it was impossible for me to hold on to any—much less all—of them. Losses continued to mount: the death of a parent and of friends, a chronic illness with the concomitant physical limitations, the horror of 9/11. All these unasked-for growth opportunities confirmed the Buddha's description of *dukkha* as being old age, illness, death, trying to get what we don't have or hold on to what we do, being with people we don't love and being separated from people we want to be with.

Much to my surprise, I learned that my addiction to everything I wanted was just as persistent as my addiction to alcohol—and had the same result: suffering. "Freedom from addiction" means freedom from addiction (clinging) to *anything*. This statement does not mean that we shouldn't have likes and preferences, merely that we shouldn't make our happiness *dependent* upon fulfilling them.

How, then, can I now say I am happy most of the time? I took my first steps toward experiencing happiness when I learned an important Dharma lesson about suffering: none of the sources of suffering is personal. They don't happen just to *me*; they happen to everyone. The more deeply I understood the universality of suffering, the easier it was for me to not cling to and identify with the sources of my suffering or to the suffering itself by telling myself stories about it.

Does this mean that I'm always giddily happy? Not at all. But much of the time I am contented (that's my "new happiness") because I try to be (mindfully) free of desiring or clinging to things that cause me suffering. When events happen that cause me pain—and there are always new surprises—I can see more clearly the conditions that led up to them, most of which are simply inherent to being born in a human body. For this reason, seeing the patterns of the past without getting caught up in them is critical.

We will not regret the past nor wish to shut the door on it.

In sobriety, my relationship to the past has gone through three main phases. First, until I had been sober for some time, I wished all my drinking life had been spent in a blackout. I didn't want to remember any of it. I wanted to "shut the door on" all the pain and humiliation that I did remember. The second phase was the acceptance that everything that had happened to me *during my drinking* was necessary for me to achieve whatever sobriety I had. In the third phase, my understanding of dependent origination and karma (Chapter 8) convinced me that for me to be who and where I am at any moment, everything that ever happened *in the world* had to have happened. Nothing is ever lost.

As painful as it was to look at the past, I found that "a searching and fearless moral inventory"—Step Four—could show me just what kind of unskillful karma I had created for myself and how I had hurt others when I acted without mindful intention. I could not live in the past, but I had to look at it. When I did, I found a life filled with repetitions of patterns that hadn't worked the first time or any subsequent times. I was literally leading a life of *re-*action, a life of re-acting out the same old unskillful karma. Seeing the pattern of such actions and reactions reinforced my motivation to cultivate mindfulness in the present so that I could create skillful karma for the future.

We will comprehend the word *serenity* and we will know peace.

The Serenity Prayer was my life mantra during early sobriety, but it took on a remarkably intense meaning for me when I saw it within the framework of the Four Noble Truths and their underlying understandings:

> Grant me the serenity to accept the things I cannot change: *the Four Noble Truths, impermanence, dependent origination, not-self, and past karma.*
> The courage to change the things I can, *by being mindful in the present moment so that my thoughts, speech, and actions will not harm myself or others now or in the future.*
> And the wisdom to know the difference *between doing what is skillful and what is unskillful.*

I was able to open the door to this penetrating understanding of serenity through the consistent practice of insight meditation, which nurtures the ability to see things as they really are (the definition of *insight*). When I could see things as they really are, the difference between the things I could change and the things I could not became clear. It was this clarity that brought me serenity, peace, and equanimity.

> No matter how far down the scale we
>   have gone, we will see how our experi-
>   ence can benefit others.
> That feeling of uselessness and self-pity
>   will disappear.
> We will lose interest in selfish things and
>   gain interest in our fellows.
> Self-seeking will slip away.

My understanding of these four promises underwent a sea-change when I finally was able to grasp the Buddhist concept of *anatta*, not-self. Although each person in a conventional sense is unique, there is no distinctive, autonomous, nonchanging entity that can be called a self. Yet how constantly and urgently we human beings indulge in the "selfing" process—the creation of a sense of unique self: We are selfing through our thoughts when we think we are better or worse or different from others and tell ourselves things like "*I* would never do anything like that" or "*I* have every right to be angry at him." We are selfing through our words when we speak just to fill an empty space and make our presence known, or brag, or lie, or say things like "It was your fault" or "You really are an idiot." Every instance when we create separation through anger, blame, or building ourselves up at others' expense is selfing. All human beings seem to need to go through selfing early in life to establish a sense of identity and to develop emotionally, but many people concretize the *I-me-my* and never seem to join the human race or recognize the interrelationship of all beings.

Alcoholics often seem to put a special spin on selfing. While our disease is active, emotionally we alcoholics have been described as "an egomaniac with an inferiority complex." For many of us, the telltale signs of alcoholism—and what I call *drunk selfing*—were evident from our earliest drinking episodes. By the time I was thirteen, very tall and looking older, I managed to put myself in many drinking situations. I didn't particularly like the taste, but I liked what alcohol made me feel: suddenly I was pretty and graceful, I wasn't freakishly tall, my hair wasn't frizzy, I could dance, I was funny, and everyone loved me. I think drinking was the only time I felt "normal" during those awful teenage years. I had an abnormally large capacity—a warning sign of alcoholism— and I took great pride in being told that I "drank like a man."

When I started drinking, I felt transformed. And I was. For whatever psychological reasons, I used alcohol to create a sense of another self because the self I had been dealt was not good enough. Sometimes I merely lied or exaggerated, but one time when I was fifteen, for an entire drunken weekend at a military academy homecoming I put on a phony French accent and claimed to be from an obscure region near Switzerland. If people spoke French to me—which I couldn't understand—I would aloofly answer, "I'm an American now, and I only speak English," and get away from them as quickly as I could. That self, frightened and desperately trying to be happy, had many years of suffering ahead.

When I got sober, one of the most challenging early tasks I faced was letting go of my "terminal uniqueness." It was hard enough, convinced that I would never have fun again, to let go of alcohol. To let go of the façade I worked so hard to maintain seemed terrifyingly difficult. Even though I was finally able to let go of drunk selfing, I immediately put sober selfing in its place.

Initially, I had to recognize that I could not get or stay sober as long as I nurtured my sense of being different. I had to become a "we" with the other people in AA. When I was able to do this, I could acknowledge that "no matter how far down the scale we had gone," I could genuinely identify with other AAs when they shared at meetings, and they could identify with me. Although the details of our stories might vary, emotionally we all had the very same story, and we benefited each other by honestly sharing and hearing that story. I gradually realized that I could identify with people outside the AA rooms in the same way—that we too had the same emotional and spiritual story.

I recognized that that all my feelings of being different and useless and all the self-pity I indulged in were products of selfing. Unfortunately, just because we learn something about ourselves doesn't mean that we can wave some kind of wand and totally change overnight. About the time I would see a selfing "strategy" clearly, another more subtle version would surface.

I used two techniques to work with selfing in a way that would not just be ways of beating up on myself: first, monitoring my emotions for any time I feel uncomfortable, and second, "noting," a technique used frequently in some forms of meditation to help focus concentration on what's going on by mentally "whispering" a word that describes what we are experiencing.

Among the many translations of the word *dukkha* are "dis-ease" and "stress." In sobriety I cultivated the habit of recognizing that I was uncomfortable—in itself a feat—and asking myself, "What's going on? Am I hungry, angry, lonely, or tired? Am I afraid? Am I angry?" The point is simply to recognize and acknowledge that something is going on—not to even ask why.

In sobriety, I used the noting technique at a macro level to identify what was happening to make me uncomfortable. A meditator may choose to use the noting technique—very softly and nonjudgmentally—to acknowledge what is happening. Some common noting during meditation are "pain, pain, pain . . . ," "restless, restless, restless . . . ," "thinking, thinking . . . ." In sobriety, when I want to identify what's happening, the notings tend to be things like "tired, tired . . . ," "threatened, threatened . . . ," "hungry, hungry . . . ."

The trick is simply to identify what is present *without* making up a story about it. When I can do that, I depersonalize the disease and stop the selfing. I can see that anger is present without pronouncing myself an angry person, with all the past and future projections my imagination can come up with about what I have done or will do. I can see that sadness is present without concretizing a sad self who will never be happy again. A powerful AA slogan is *Feelings Are Not Facts*, and noting is a constructive way to acknowledge that the emotions are there without endowing them with a sense of permanence. When we can see that feelings of uselessness and self-pity are present and that they are not facts, we can let go of them—and they disappear.

When we are able to see the impermanence of the feelings that we get so wrapped up in, it becomes increasingly easy to let go of them—"to lose interest in selfish things." We can see that just as we can get caught up in selfing, so do those around us. We learn to remember that just as our selfing is impermanent, so is theirs. In this way, we can allow ourselves to be truly in and with the present moment and can open to others without the dualistic judgmentalism we usually use to drive wedges between us, and we can take genuine interest in them.

As we learn more and more about the many and mindless ways we indulge in selfing, we increasingly realize the pointlessness of it. "Self-seeking will slip away" because we are able to acknowledge our interconnection with all other beings, as well as the fact that whatever we may seek will pass away, leaving us suffering again if we cling to it.

Our whole attitude and outlook upon life will change.

Recognizing our interconnectedness with others dramatically changes our attitude and outlook upon life. We begin in sobriety by identifying—not comparing—with the other people who are seeking recovery. If we stay sober and continue to work the AA program, we discover that it truly is a "bridge back to life." AA is a safe place for us to make ourselves vulnerable to others and to learn the joy of unconditional love. Gradually, we begin to open ourselves to those people outside of AA with whom we regularly interact—our families, friends, coworkers. Eventually, we find that we can extend the same openness to others whom we may know only slightly or not at all.

When, through the Dharma, we glimpse the meaning of the challenging concept that we are empty of a separate self, we come to realize that so is everyone and *everything* else. At that point, we become a gem in the mythical Indra's net: According to Vedic mythology, King Indra ordered his architects to erect a net around the entire universe with a precious jewel at every junction; in this way every jewel reflected, and was reflected in, every other jewel. When we are able to see ourselves in all others and see all others in ourselves, a life transformation occurs that is propelled by wisdom and compassion for all others. We will understand in a new way how anonymity is the spiritual foundation of all that we do.

Fear of people and of economic insecurity will leave us.

This promise refers to a generalized social/emotional fear of people—not to the very sensible fear that might arise in confrontation with, say, an axe murderer. When we come to understand anonymity and our interconnectedness with others, we are able to let go of fear of them. In its place, we experience compassion, the genuine empathic understanding of why others act in ways that seem threatening to us. We know that they are selfing. We understand that our fear may also be a form of selfing (unless we are objectively in a situation of imminent danger).

Further, experiencing fear is not being in the present moment but arises because of something that *may* happen. Usually we are afraid that people *will in the future* reject us because we're not clever enough, or smart enough, or attractive enough, or something-else enough. When we hold on strongly to such fears, we tend to isolate. And because our actions begin in our mind, when we are with the people we fear we probably will act in a way that makes our fear into a self-fulfilling prophecy.

When I first began going to AA, my sponsor told me I had to introduce myself to three people at each meeting and to see if there was a group going out for coffee after the meeting that I could join. Frightened and certain of rejection, I would go up to someone and hostilely say, "You don't want to go out to coffee do you?" Of course they didn't. I kept setting myself up. I finally learned to rephrase the question to, "Is anyone going out to coffee?" More often than not I would be invited to join people who may not have even planned to go out. Similarly, it is very common for newcomers in AA to get people's telephone numbers and get in the habit of calling supportive people. When I told my sponsor that I was afraid of the phone, she suggested that when the AA member answers the phone, I say, "Hi, this is Laura. I'm practicing." The AA member I'd called would understand my nervousness and immediately take the lead in the conversation.

In both situations—asking to go for coffee and calling—AA members who knew nothing about Buddhism were able to respond because they had heartfelt interconnectedness to other people in recovery. After I had been sober for a while, I was able to ask newcomers to join me for coffee and answer phone calls from them without the slightest twinge of nervousness, much less fear. It was a clear example of the impermanence of emotions, as I came to see when I got involved in the Dharma.

Before I got sober and in early sobriety, I felt as if any emotion that arose for me would last forever. I had genuine economic insecurity—I was getting short-term disability payments but was too muddled from the shock treatments to see my situation clearly. When I went out for coffee after AA meetings, I'd buy a cup (it was much cheaper then!) but not order any food. Instead, I'd ask people who got sandwiches if they were going to eat their pickles. For about a year, I ate rice and vegetables at home, and pickles were my big treat when I went out. (Needless to say, I hardly ever eat them now.)

I was well into the Dharma the next time the occasion for financial insecurity arose. I was quite amazed by my own response to it. I knew that my challenging financial situation was not personal—many people lose jobs. I knew that it was not permanent— I had worked my way up the career ladder once in sobriety and knew that I could again, if I chose to, starting on a much higher rung than the first time. I knew that I'd be sad but all right if I had to give up my apartment and material things, which were impermanent anyway. In an interesting twist resulting from my appreciation of the Buddhist teachings on wise livelihood, I fearlessly made a decision that on the surface prolonged my "financial insecurity": I turned down jobs immediately offered because my industry was changing so much that it was no longer possible for me to play the management role I had previously held in a way that was nonharming in the broadest sense of the term.

It became clear to me, in fact, that I had been fired because I had refused to implement corporate practices that harmed others. I had the luxury of severance pay, which enabled me to continue for a while living at much the same level although I chose to do a kind of freelance work that paid me about one quarter of what I had been earning. When the time came that I could no longer live where and how I had in the past because of my own decision, I was able to make the necessary changes without fear. But not without grief—I felt very sad to move away from the things, places, people, and AA meetings that had been comfortable and comforting to me for years. The Dharma understanding that I could never hold on to anything permanently anyway eased the sting as I made the life changes my karmic decision entailed. (An aside: There was neither an AA group nor a sangha in the mountain town I moved to . . . so I started both.)

We will intuitively know how to handle situations that used to baffle us.

The changes I described above are a dramatic example of coming to know how to intuitively handle such situations. While I was drinking, I reacted to baffling situations rather than responding with the intuition that insight brings. Simply being sober enabled me to deal with many situations I would previously have tried to avoid. When I came to understand the profound implications of karma as taught by the Buddha, my choices in how to handle perplexing situations became clearer and I made decisions with greater confidence.

When I decided to leave a traditional career, I did something for myself that I had previously done many times with business groups: I did a strategic plan—this time for my life rather than some company's product line. It had all the same components—goals, plans, finances, a timeline, and the hardest part of any strategic plan to formulate: a mission statement. Usually, a mission statement will say something like "The mission of Company X is to create and market innovative widgets in order to claim a 12 percent market share with a gross margin of 40 percent within five years."

I repeatedly—without any luck—tried to formulate a mission statement about what I wanted to *do* but had no success at all until I realized that I had to put what I wanted to *be* into the equation. Instead of my old description of "I am what I do," I had to turn the emphasis around to "I do what I am." I was finally able to devise the mission statement I sought: "I will live a sober life of nonharming." The supporting plans included attending AA meetings and Buddhist meditation retreats and committing to studying the Dharma. In terms of finances, I determined how much money I needed to earn in order to support my mission, and I developed business plans to pay my expenses.

I have intuitively known how to handle every situation since then, whether work, social, or personal. The guidelines have been clear and simple and have come down to the answers to two questions: "Does this move me toward rather than away from a drink?" *and* "Will this harm anyone—including myself—in any way?" I try to think, act, and speak in ways so that I can categorically answer, "No," to *both* questions.

**We will suddenly realize that God is doing for us
what we could not do for ourselves.**

The day I was able to face my alcoholism, I realized that a Group of Drunks was doing for me something I could not do for myself: helping me to get and stay sober. But I was not fully able to fulfill the Big Book description of a recovering alcoholic as skipping along on the road of destiny happy, joyous, and free. In so many ways, all of these things had happened, but I kept hitting patches of unhappiness that I couldn't quite understand. I thought I must not be working the AA program right. On the outside, my life looked great—and it was—but there was the nagging question "Is this all there is?" It was the same question the Buddha-to-be had asked when he began his spiritual quest. It was a question that played a large role in my seeking a spiritual path, which turned out to be Buddhism, in addition to the Twelve Steps.

As I described in Chapter 11, study of the Dharma led me to realize that the Higher Power—the greatest power—for me was the ability to bring mindfulness to all aspects of my life. When I am mindful, I am kind, I am honest, and I am moving away from a drink. By developing mindfulness through the practice of insight meditation, I act with the understandings of impermanence, not-self, and suffering. Increasingly I am truly happy, joyous, and free in my sober life because, in finding the Middle Path espoused by the Buddha, I am able to blend the AA program and the Dharma seamlessly. The more I have been able to bring together the two most important elements of my life without compromising either, the more I have been awestruck with gratitude for both.

14

SUBLIME
ABIDING

IN THE BUDDHA'S time, "sojourning places" called *viharas* were established where monks on pilgrimage or spreading the Dharma could rest and meditate. So that we too might have a "place" to sojourn in peace, the Buddha taught four "sublime states" called the *Brahma-viharas* ("Divine Abodes") that we could use as the object of meditation and practice. The place is in our heart-mind, and practicing the *Brahma-viharas* can concentrate our minds and at the same time open our hearts to the four sublime states: lovingkindness, compassion, sympathetic joy, and equanimity. When we can dwell in these abodes, we indeed can come to know a very special sublime abiding in sobriety.

In my experience, the *Brahma-viharas* flow directly from three AA promises: *We will lose interest in selfish things and gain interest in our fellows*; *Self-seeking will slip away*; and *Our whole attitude and outlook upon life will change*. The *Brahma-vihara* practices are extremely forceful means of reinforcing these promises in our daily lives.

When we become involved with AA's Twelve Steps and promises for a sober life, we focus on each one until we can internalize it—add it to our toolbox for daily living. We can learn to practice the *Brahma-viharas* the same way. The ultimate goal is identical within the context of AA and of the Dharma: to "practice these principles in all our affairs."

LOVINGKINDNESS/*METTA*

The formal practice of lovingkindness (*metta* in Pali) is undertaken as a concentration practice, but it also has the transformative effect of opening us to boundless feelings of friendship and affection for ourselves and other beings. In addition, the Buddha defined *metta* as a practice that protects against any kind of fear. In this sphere, it works for me much the same way that prayer did in early sobriety. My sponsor told me that if I persistently prayed, I could get through the roughest situations that made me want to drink. Indeed, praying worked, though as I noted earlier, I never knew whether I simply couldn't keep two things in my mind at once (the prayer and the threat) or if Honey Pie was listening and helping. When we are particularly mentally or physically restless, *metta* may be a more effective concentration practice than sitting meditation because at such times we may be able to focus more deeply on words than on our breath.

Lovingkindness is an important part of my daily practice. I use it when I'm sitting on my cushion, but also when I'm in frustrating situations such as standing in a checkout line at a store or sitting in a traffic jam. I also turn to lovingkindness when I encounter a person or group to whom I have aversive reactions—a coworker who is being aggressive, a loudmouth spouting political opinions I disagree with, a child or pet who is nagging me to play when I'm trying to finish an important task. When I (am willing to) direct these phrases to the challenging person, my heart softens, I relax, and I can deal with the situation in a way that I won't later regret.

A caution: We can't expect to feel emotional waves of lovingkindness wash over us when we begin to do *metta* practice. The point is to use it as a concentration practice, not as a bliss trip. If we practice *metta* with consistency, at some point warm emotions will arise and we will realize that the practice has stealthily enabled us to care—sometimes very deeply—about people we may not even know.

We practice *metta* by selecting and silently repeating (usually) four phrases that express the kinds of good things we would wish for ourselves and for others we love. The phrases may be complex or as simple as these:

> *May I be happy.*
> *May I be healthy.*
> *May I live safely.*
> *May I be free.*

We say the phrases to ourselves over and over, with a slight pause after each one so we can imagine what that particular condition would feel like to ourselves or to the person to whom we send the wish. When our attention wanders, as it does in all kinds of meditation, we simply reel our awareness back to the present moment and return to reciting the phrases.

In traditional lovingkindness practice, we direct these phrases to specific categories of beings in a fixed order: oneself, a spiritual benefactor, a friend, a neutral person, a difficult person, and finally all beings everywhere. In theory (at least in Asia 2,600 years ago) we move from the easiest being (ourself) to the most challenging (all beings).

How long we spend on each category—ten minutes, an hour, a month, a year—depends on the circumstances in which we are using this practice. Some meditators use *metta* as their entire practice. Some go on *metta* retreats and practice intensively for days, weeks, or months. I and many others begin or end a meditation sitting with lovingkindness phrases. Note that "aiming" the phrases at all the categories is usually done in *formal* practice, but when we use *metta* as all or part of a daily practice, we may direct lovingkindness to only one or several beings, such as a friend going through a difficult time or someone who is ill, or to all beings caught in warfare or all beings everywhere.

It's very difficult to generate wishes of lovingkindness while we're hanging on to resentments, so many people spiritually "cleanse their palate" by doing a forgiveness contemplation before a formal period of lovingkindnness practice. The common forgiveness phrases that I usually repeat several times each, reflecting on their meaning, are as follows:

If anyone has harmed me intentionally or unintentionally
by word, thought, or deed, may I forgive them.
If I have harmed anyone intentionally or unintentionally by
word, thought, or deed, may they forgive me.
If I have harmed myself intentionally or unintentionally by
word, thought, or deed, may I forgive myself.

Sometimes, especially when I first began lovingkindness practice, I have devoted a specific period (often a week) to doing *metta* within the context of AA. When I do "AA Metta," the phrases have had varying meanings. But I always begin with forgiveness contemplation. Here's how I direct my awareness during that time:

Anyone who has harmed me . . . For an alcoholic, holding on to a resentment against someone, in words often heard at AA meetings, is like taking poison and expecting the other person to die. When I don't let go, the acid of anger is in my stomach, not theirs. AA members are often encouraged to pray for someone against whom they hold a resentment. I actually find working with this forgiveness phrase easier than praying for someone, because it seems wiser to me to express the desire/intention to forgive the other person(s) *for my own well-being* and so that I will not act unskillfully toward him or her in the future.

Anger, blame, and resentment are wedges between people, and the duality created goes against the spiritual practices I undertake in order to experience the interconnectedness of all beings. If there is a particular person who harmed me while I was drinking, I usually bring to mind that person. Otherwise, I express the intention to forgive anyone who harmed me during my years of drinking—and recovery—remembering, as I noted in Chapter 3, that I often played the role of compliant victim.

Anyone I have harmed . . . Sometimes guilt has lingered for me over my actions toward someone while I was drinking although I have made "direct amends" in working Step 9. For example, during my drinking years I committed many "sins of omission" toward my mother by simply being absent at times when my presence was important to her. If I'm still holding on to a pain like that, I bring the specific person to mind. Otherwise, I direct this wish to "all I harmed while drinking" because I can never really know the extent of the harm I created. Sometimes I preface the phrase with an acknowledgment such as "Knowing that I am a child of the universe, still trying to recover from my addiction, may anyone I have harmed, directly or indirectly . . ."

If I have harmed myself . . . During all the years of my active addiction I harmed myself, however unintentionally, by my thoughts, words, and actions on a daily basis. My sponsor insisted that I put myself at the top of my Step Nine amends list because I had harmed no one as much as myself and needed to make amends to no one as much as to myself. Every day of recovery is such an amend, but I find that to forgive myself I've needed to actively remember that my harmful acts were symptomatic of the disease of alcoholism. Although I must take responsibility for my actions—then and now—I must not continue to beat myself up over something in the past. I must forgive myself rather than wallow in the distraction of guilt and get on with making things right ("amending") in the present.

Having earnestly contemplated forgiveness, I am ready to begin sending lovingkindness to various groups of beings. The phrases I use take on particular meaning for me within the context of AA:

May I be happy. May I recognize and be grateful for all the miraculous gifts of my sobriety.

May I be healthy. May I recover physically, mentally, and spiritually.

May I live safely. May I be safe from outside dangers, including seductive drinking situations, but also from internal dangers such as the manifestations of the Five Hindrances, especially desire (for a mood-changing chemical).

May I be free. May I be liberated from the control of addiction but also from the sense of self that separates me from others.

Revisiting the list of people to whom we direct these phrases:

Oneself. Just as my sponsor told me that no one was more deserving of my forgiveness than I was myself, the Buddha said that no one is more deserving of our good wishes than we are ourselves, so we should begin with ourselves because doing so would be the easiest place to start. Maybe for him—but not necessarily for a recovering alcoholic who may still have dark corners of guilt and self-loathing. For many people in recovery, beginning with one-self—even after doing the forgiveness contemplation—can be very challenging.

One way that can ease this pain is to direct the phrases to ourself before our addiction took hold either by visualizing or by looking at an actual photograph of ourself during a happy time, perhaps during childhood, and sending lovingkindness to the person in that image. Healing may take time—sometimes a very long time—but gradually our heart will soften toward ourselves and we'll be able to send the good wishes to ourselves in the present moment and mean it.

If we experience great suffering when we try to send lovingkindness to ourselves even while directing it to an image of a happier time, another possibility is to send *metta* to ourselves and our spiritual benefactor at the same time: "May we be happy, may we be healthy, may we live safely, may we be free." If this too is very painful, we should back off and move on to the next category. Remember, *metta* is first and foremost a concentration practice, and if we experience extremely difficult emotions while practicing, the result is counterproductive.

After we become comfortable sending lovingkindness to ourselves, the practice is an extremely helpful tool to rely on when things get very rough emotionally or even physically. I've known several people who have eased suffering while healing from surgeries and chemotherapy by sending themselves *metta*. It doesn't work to send *metta* to a painful incision and expect the pain to go away, because that focus may cause contraction and possibly more pain, but it does help to repeat these good wishes to the whole being who is suffering: ourselves. *Metta* can also be an emotional "quick fix" when we find ourselves in an unexpected difficult spot.

Spiritual benefactor. When I'm doing "regular" *metta*, I usually use the Dalai Lama as my spiritual benefactor because he always inspires me to persist on my spiritual path; on a daily basis he is my role model for the qualities I would like to cultivate. Occasionally I use one or more of the Buddhist teachers with whom I study. Most days, I meditate while sitting in front of a small home altar on which I have placed photographs of the Dalai Lama and my teachers. I look at these images as I send lovingkindness to them and usually end up with warm feelings in my heart and a broad grin on my face.

On the occasions when I am practicing lovingkindness specifically as an extension and support of my AA program, I use my first sponsor or all the sponsors I've had as my spiritual benefactor. In Theravada Buddhism (my tradition), Dharma teachers are often referred to by the Pali word *kalyanamitta*, "spiritual friend." The Buddha maintained that the whole of spiritual life for his monks is comradeship with like-minded seekers.

With very rare exception, our sponsors truly fulfill this role of patient, supportive, and comforting spiritual guides who are steadfastly there for us, to help us learn how to recover one day at a time and to "practice these [AA] principles in all our affairs." There is no way that I could ever repay directly the generosity of my AA sponsors (though I do so indirectly every time I sponsor a newcomer), but I can acknowledge it in a heartfelt way by sending them wishes for happiness, health, safety, and freedom when I do *metta*. On the times I've had difficulty sending lovingkindness to myself, I have imagined sitting with my sponsor and sending it to both of us. I feel safe and loved by and deeply connected to another being, and the warmest possible loving feelings flow.

Friend. For this person, it is best to choose someone who is not of the gender that attracts us. *Metta* is a concentration practice, and if we are sending lovingkindness to a person with whom we have a complex relationship, we can be greatly distracted by feelings of desire, a very different emotion. Usually when I'm doing this phase of *metta* I use a close friend or sometimes my dog. Many people use a grandchild. Both pets and grandchildren are also fine to use in "AA Metta," but more often I use a particular program friend or members of a particular AA group as my friend. I like to meditate with others because their energy and commitment to sitting for a full period has helped me not to give up when I've felt especially tired or discouraged with my practice.

Sober AA members have played the same role for me. When I feel too tired to go to a meeting, I know that all my "friends" will be there, waiting for me, and will worry if I don't show up. I show up. Particularly in early sobriety, when waves of doubt washed over me and I was sure that I couldn't stay sober another day, friends at meetings (or on the telephone) gave me the support and hope I needed to get through the bad patch. When I was so contracted by emotional pain that I could not ask for help, watching others make themselves vulnerable gave me the courage to reach out. My recovery and my spiritual quest have both been supported and enhanced by friends, and I can ardently wish for them health, happiness, and freedom.

Neutral person. Early in my practice of lovingkindess, working with a neutral person made me extremely uncomfortable—primarily because my judging mind jumped up at first contact and I did not actually feel neutral toward anyone. I often used a supermarket checkout person at a lane I didn't regularly stand in or, on retreats, someone sitting ahead of me whose face I had not seen. I heard many stories of how practitioners had come to love a gardener or vacuum cleaner repair person, but I felt that the time spent on this category was pretty much wasted for me.

A major block was that even though I had been told not to anticipate instantly developing warm and fuzzy feelings, I somehow *did* expect them. I felt as if I wasn't making any progress because they didn't envelop me—until the day that the checkout person or the retreatant was not in their usual place and I found myself looking around for them. I had learned to be concerned without knowing it.

I had a remarkable change in relationship to this category when I realized that "my" neutral person was a surrogate for all the beings in the world that I do not know. I was then able to practice ardently, strengthening my interconnectedness with all beings everywhere by sending them lovingkindess. In AA Metta the neutral person, for me, stands in for all the anonymous alcoholics in the world—struggling or sober—to whom I am connected through the disease of alcoholism. I focus on a specific person as proxy, through whom I direct lovingkindness to all alcoholics.

Difficult person. In dealing with a difficult person, sometimes referred to as The Enemy in classical practice, it is very helpful to focus on the fact that, with the possible exception of deeply ill sociopaths, truly happy people do not intentionally harm others, and even sociopaths do so because of their own heavy karma and are thus worthy of our *metta* as well. To the extent that beings are consumed by greed, hatred, and delusion/ignorance they are suffering in equivalent measure and express their suffering by acting against others. When I was learning lovingkindness practice, my teachers urged me to not choose the most difficult person I had ever encountered but rather to use someone who was merely an *irritant.*

For many years, every day I went into my office and practiced lovingkindness toward an extremely unpleasant coworker—with the result that we worked together compatibly for about five years longer than I could ever have imagined. (Ironically, he turned out to be an alcoholic, and his disease was the source of much of his disagreeableness. An important lesson.) I've also frequently focused *metta* on a political leader whose positions create in me great aversion.

In developing a lovingkindness practice within the context of AA, it's helpful to begin with someone who annoys us at meetings—talks too much, slurps coffee, or always comes late and leaves early. If we have the opportunity before meetings begin, for example, we should sit where we can see "our" person and send lovingkindness, pausing after each phrase to imagine how the person would feel if he or she was happy, healthy, safe, and free. No matter how much *metta* we send to annoying people, they probably won't change—but we will. And when we change, we will treat them differently, and they may in fact begin to change. A woman with whom I eventually became friendly once said to me, "Ten years ago you were the only person who would talk to me." She was someone to whom I had been sending lovingkindness.

After some years of practicing AA Metta, I now tend to pick as "my" difficult person someone who disturbs my serenity in a way that could be a threat to my sobriety, no matter how slight. For me, this practice has worked in the most painful situation I've faced in sobriety. A long-term relationship ended in a way that devastated me and brought up grief, rage, fear, desire for revenge—in words, all kinds of unskillful emotions. One of my teachers insisted that I begin and continue a concentrated *metta* practice until I could hold my ex in my heart. My teacher also added, "But this doesn't mean that you ever have to have your ex in your house again."

I'm not saying that I no longer have piercing grief over this loss—sometimes it comes at unexpected moments and I feel as if

I am going to contract with pain until I implode. At those times, I force myself to start cranking out *metta* phrases, and the *dukkha* eases. Just as I have sometimes imagined myself with my spiritual benefactor and sent lovingkindnessto us both, at particularly difficult times I send *metta* simultaneously to me and my ex, acknowledging the suffering that we both bear.

All beings everywhere, in all realms, without exception. After the difficult person, the group of "all beings everywhere" sometimes seems like a great relief. I find that it's easiest for me to "organize" these beings in schematics—for example, to use the six directions and see who comes up: "all beings above" (birds, insects, people in the space station, beings in other worlds if there are any, etc.); "all beings below" (worms, insects, moles, sea life, miners, etc.); "to the north" (Inuits, Canadians, Scandinavians, polar bears, elk, etc.); "to the south" (Mexicans, Central and South Americans, Africans, Australians and New Zealanders, penguins, orcas, Antarctic researchers, etc.); "to the east" (Europeans, people in Iceland and Newfoundland, people living in warring areas in the Middle East); "to the west" (Pacific Islanders, Asians, yaks, pandas, etc.). Sometimes my geographic wandering lands me somewhere that I remain for quite a while, such as sending lovingkindness to starving people uprooted by "ethnic cleansing" in Sudan; to the suffering people of Iraq or Palestine or Israel; to the military people who have been separated from their families and sent to places where intentionally or not they may inflict suffering on others and may be the objects of violence. I wish them all safety, health, happiness, and freedom.

Another way I might divide up the universe was suggested by a Sri Lankan teacher: all beings with no legs, with two legs, with four legs, with six legs, with many legs. This scheme works well sometimes, but other times I get stuck—for example, "no legs" (Do I really want to send *metta* to the microbes causing my cold?) or "two legs" (Isn't it strange that this grouping comprises primates and birds?). Instead of repeating the phrases, I end up thinking about whether all microbes play a constructive role in the world or evolution. I try to end the train of thought by saying, "Well, they just want to be happy too, whatever that means for them. We all want to be happy but do things that cause ourselves and others suffering." Enter thoughts of antibiotics and genetic mutations because of environmental damage, and I'm gone again.

When I do AA Metta for all beings, I send these wishes to all alcoholics in the world—sober or still struggling—and the loved ones who have been affected by their disease, two categories that cover just about everyone. So many images of my own and friends' experiences flicker through the back of my consciousness that unbounded gratitude for my own recovery wells up and I fervently want others who suffer to have what I have been given. My heart-mind passionately sends wishes of lovingkindness throughout the world to all anonymous alcoholics.

COMPASSION / *KARUNA*

One Buddhist teacher defined *compassion* (*karuna* in Pali) as the quivering of the heart in response to another's pain. I had always thought of compassion as feeling sorry for others and trying to help them whenever possible. As I studied the Dharma I learned about "near enemies"—which may resemble skillful states, such as one of the *Brahma-viharas*, but are not and in fact can lead us into unskillful thoughts, words, and actions. Many times when I thought I was being compassionate, I instead was expressing *pity*, an emotional set that creates separation between others and ourselves rather than creating interconnectedness because at some level we believe that the Others are somehow different from, even below, us.

Learning about compassion in sobriety was a rocky road for me. In my New York City neighborhood, I encountered panhandlers on almost every corner. I averted my eyes and walked past them, often as they called out to me, "Please help me get something to eat." I felt sorry for them—poor *them*—but there was no way I'd give them money because I was sure they were all alcoholics and drug addicts and I didn't want to enable them to buy booze and drugs. My withholding was good for them, wasn't it? It felt terrible.

So every day as I walked home from my office—about 20 minutes away—I bought a bunch of bananas from a street vendor and distributed them to everyone who asked me for money. Some of the panhandlers were genuinely happy to have the fruit, but I tended to remember only the one who threw it back at me. The lesson I began to learn through the Dharma was that spontaneity is a critical ingredient in generosity. If I had to stop and think about what people might use my gift for or whether or not they would be adequately grateful, I was not experiencing or expressing generosity. I continued to buy bananas for the walk home, but I began to also carry a pocketful of quarters too and to give one to whoever asked me for money before I offered them fruit.

My next step was to *look at* the people who asked me for money, to make eye contact except when the person was clearly mentally ill and might respond to eye contact with hostility. When I could look panhandlers in the eye, they became human beings, just like me, and I could experience that quivering of the heart that is truly compassion. Sometimes I gave more than a quarter. Once I took a woman with an infant into a market to buy diapers and formula. Sometimes I got "took," but I didn't mind, because having a more open heart was worth so much more to me than money.

Usually, compassion practice is done using one phrase, rather than four, as in practicing *metta*. The phrase I use most often is "May you be free of suffering." Although I have done formal periods of compassion practice, repeatedly directing the phrase to the same groups I use in practicing lovingkindness, most often I do it informally and as spontaneously as I would hope to feel generosity or compassion should I see someone who is in pain. I find that I send compassionate wishes for the end of suffering to almost everyone who shares at an AA meeting. I even catch myself extending *karuna* to people I see on television. Since this practice is about cultivating compassion in oneself, there's no contradiction in sending it to any being, in person or otherwise, who evokes it.

Since moving from New York City, I have fewer opportunities to "practice" compassion. I use it in many of the same type situations as lovingkindness, but because it is briefer, I tend to use it where there is a situation of spontaneity (such as driving past a group of obviously drunk men leaving a dilapidated bar) but I use *metta* with more foresight and intention.

There is not much difference for me between general expressions of compassion and those directed to someone suffering from or affected by alcoholism. I have found that *karuna* practice is cumulative, and the compassionate quivering of the heart and wishes for suffering to end occur more and more spontaneously. Its effects are remarkable in breaking down a sense of separation between ourselves and others, alcoholic or not.

SYMPATHETIC JOY/*MUDITA*

The response of sympathetic joy (*mudita* in Pali) to others' or even our own good fortune is difficult for anyone caught up in selfing, but it sometimes seems especially challenging for alcoholics. When we go to AA meetings and hear people describing a new job or a great vacation or a healed family relationship, we may unexpectedly be buffeted by unskillful emotions such as doubt, jealousy, and anger. It's as if their happiness is somehow directed *at* us to make us feel bad—as if what happened to them had some quantitative relationship to our quota of good fortune, which of course it doesn't. We find ourselves thinking things like "A creep like him doesn't deserve it"; "I should have that by now because I've been sober longer than her"; "With all that good luck, he'll probably get drunk"; "Good things happen for everyone but me— what did I do wrong?"

The longer we're sober, the more able we are to be happy for others, but that state often doesn't come easily or quickly. It requires, first, realizing that our sobriety is the result of the steps that we take one day at a time, and the good things promised in the book *Alcoholics Anonymous* will come as our unbroken recovery unfolds.

Second, we come to understand that our own self-centeredness is getting in the way of feeling happiness for others and that the things that will make us happy will come too at the karmically right times in our recovery. We then can consciously and sincerely practice sympathetic joy when good things come to others by repeating a phrase such as "May I find joy in your success" even as the situation presents itself.

For some recovering alcoholics, a sad parallel to envy of others' successes is that often we cannot be happy for *our own* good fortune. At some deep level we may still be filled with self-loathing or guilt and feel that we may not deserve it. Another common response is to not trust the good luck and to fear that we will lose "it"—the new job or car or relationship—and we set ourselves up to do just that. The Dharma can help a lot in both these types of situations. Before we actually practice *mudita*, we may need to spend some time contemplating or practicing a different skill. In the situation where bad feelings for ourselves are a problem, we can practice directing *metta* toward ourselves. When the Buddha said that no one was more deserving of lovingkindness than we are, he didn't add that we nevertheless shouldn't have good fortune or be happy.

Fear that we will lose whatever good things come to us is one of the classic explanations for the origin of *dukkha*, the Second Noble Truth. When we come to understand that making our happiness dependent upon something impermanent and clinging to it can only bring suffering, we can acknowledge impermanence, use our understanding to try to avoid clinging, and probably not do the things that would force loss.

With some clarity about why we have trouble taking joy in our successes, we can intentionally practice cultivating *mudita* by repeating phrases such as "May I find joy in my success." Because the world is created through our mind's intentions, we can cultivate sympathetic joy for both others and ourselves by practicing it earnestly.

EQUANIMITY/*UPEKKHA*

Equanimity (*upekkha* in Pali) is both a goal and a result of practicing the AA program together with the Dharma teachings in all aspects of our lives. With equanimity, we can face the ever-changing circumstances—sometimes easy, sometimes difficult—of our daily lives because we understand the nature of reality, including our own alcoholism. I expressed this principle in my "enhanced" first line of the Serenity Prayer:

> Grant me the serenity to accept the things I cannot change: *the Four Noble Truths, impermanence, dependent origination, not-self, and past karma.*

The reality we come to understand is knowable and is reliable because it is "lawful."

When we grasp the reality of the existence, cause, and cessation of *dukkha*, we will not take personally the inevitable suffering that comes into our lives. We can see it for what it is and is not, and we can use both the Dharma and the AA program to help us deal with it.

Instead of being threatened by the prospect of change, we will comprehend that impermanence is the natural way of things and beings, unavoidable. In AA we were told, "If you do not change, you will drink again." In fact, we have no choice—we *will* change whether we want to or not. But we can see that if we are mindfully present in the moment, we can shape those changes: we can create "good" karma for ourselves. We can see that everything in our sober world depends on everything else, and we have the tools to see whether we are moving toward or away from a drink, toward or away from happiness and liberation.

Finally, those of us who spent so many years imprisoned by "the disease of isolation" join in as an integral facet of the world even as we understand that we do not exist apart from it. In our sobriety we join the human race and with equanimity are one with all beings everywhere.

WORKS CITED
AND
SUGGESTED
READINGS

ALCOHOLICS ANONYMOUS

Alcoholics Anonymous, 4th edition. New York: Alcoholics Anonymous World Services, Inc., 2001.

Alcoholics Anonymous Comes of Age: A Brief History of A.A. New York: Alcoholics Anonymous World Services, Inc., 1957.

Living Sober. New York: Alcoholics Anonymous World Services, Inc., 1975.

Twelve Steps and Twelve Traditions. New York: Alcoholics Anonymous World Services, Inc., 1953.

BUDDHISM

Dalai Lama, His Holiness. *The Four Noble Truths*. London: Thorsons, 1997.

Goldstein, Joseph, and Jack Kornfield. *Seeking the Heart of Wisdom: The Path of Insight Meditation*. Boston: Shambhala, 1987.

Gunaratana, Venerable Henepola. *Eight Mindful Steps to Happiness*. Boston: Wisdom Publications, 2001.

———. *Mindfulness in Plain English*. Boston: Wisdom Publications, 1991.

Kornfield, Jack. *A Path with Heart: A Guide Through the Perils and Promises of Spiritual Life*. New York: Bantam Books, 1993.

Nanamoli, Bhikkhu, and Bhikkhu Bodhi. *The Middle-Length Discourses of the Buddha (Majjhima Nikaya)*. Boston: Wisdom Publications, 1995.

Nhat Hanh, Thich. *Old Path White Clouds: Walking in the Footsteps of the Buddha*. Berkeley: Parallax Press, 1991.

Salzberg, Sharon. *Lovingkindness: The Revolutionary Art of Happiness*. Boston: Shambhala, 1995.

Smith, Jean. *NOW! The Art of Being Truly Present*. Boston: Wisdom Publications, 2004.

———. *The Beginner's Guide to Walking the Buddha's Eightfold Path*. New York: Bell Tower, 2002.

Thanissaro Bhikkhu, trans. *Dhammapada*. Barre, MA: Dhamma Dana Publications, 1998.

BRIEF GLOSSARY OF SELECTED TERMS IN BUDDHISM

---

aggregates (*skandhas* in Sanskrit; *khandhas* in Pali) the five components the Buddha said constitute a human being: material form (body); feeling (the quality of pleasantness, unpleasantness, or neither pleasantness nor unpleasantness); perception; mental formations (thoughts, emotions, or mental qualities such as love, anger, and mindfulness); and consciousness (which arises when contact is made with one of our sense doors so that there is visual, auditory, nasal, gustatory, tactile, or mind consciousness)

anatta *See* not-self

Brahma-viharas See Divine Abodes

Buddha (Pali, Sanskrit) "Awakened One"; the historical figure probably born during the sixth century BCE (563–483 BCE?) into the Shakya clan, in what is now Nepal, and given the name Siddhartha Gautama (Sanskrit; Siddhatta Gotama, Pali); also known as the Shakyamuni Buddha ("the Buddha of the Shakya clan")

buddha (Pali, Sanskrit) "awakened one," a fully enlightened being

compassion (*karuna* in Pali) the "quivering of the heart" in response to pain and suffering

concentration the mind gathered and directed toward an object; one-pointedness of mind

dependent origination the twelve karmic links the Buddha used to describe how *dukkha* arises and can be ended: ignorance, mental formations, consciousness, mentality-materiality, six sense bases, contact, feeling, craving, clinging, becoming, birth, *dukkha*

Dhammapada an early collection of the Buddha's sayings in verse

Dharma (Sanskrit; Dhamma in Pali) when capitalized, the Buddha's teachings; most often referred to by the Sanskrit term in the West; when lowercased, any manifestation of reality— any *thing*—any object of thought

Divine Abodes (*Brahma-viharas* in Pali, Sanskrit) absorptive meditation practice directed toward lovingkindness (*metta* in Pali; *maitri* in Sanskrit), compassion (*karuna*), sympathetic joy (*mudita*), and equanimity (*upekkha* in Pali; *upeksha* in Sanskrit)

dukkha (Pali, Sanskrit) the quality of underlying stress, dissatisfaction, discomfort, and impatience that is part of everyday life and can cause suffering when there is no wisdom; most often translated as "suffering"

Eightfold Path the Fourth Noble Truth; the Buddha's teachings on how to end *dukkha* (suffering) through wise understanding, wise thought, wise speech, wise livelihood, wise effort, wise mindfulness, and wise concentration

enlightenment to see into the true nature of reality, including our own; to be free of all greed, hatred, and delusion, including the sense of a separate self; *nirvana*

equanimity (*upekkha* in Pali) accepting how things are without grasping or aversion

feeling in the context of Buddhism, the affective component of whether a sensation is pleasant, unpleasant, or neutral

First Noble Truth *dukkha* (unsatisfactoriness) is the intrinsic nature of existence

Five Hindrances five qualities that challenge mindfulness and meditation and obscure our freedom: desire (clinging), ill will (aversion), sloth and torpor (drowsiness), restlessness (mental or physical), and doubt

Four Noble Truths the heart of the Buddha's teaching—that *dukkha* is part of our lives; that it has a cause; that it can be ended; that the method for ending *dukkha* is the Eightfold Path

Fourth Noble Truth the way to end *dukkha* through the Eightfold Path

impermanence (*anicca* in Pali; *anitya* in Sanskrit) the fact that all things pass away, the root cause of all *dukkha*

insight the ability to see clearly things as they really are

Insight Meditation the name used in the West for Theravada Buddhism practice; also called Vipassana; the Buddha's practical teachings for awakening, which allows us to live without suffering

karma (Sanskrit; *kamma* in Pali) "action" or "deed"; our conscious intentions, thoughts, words, and actions, which affect results in both the present and the future

Mahayana Buddhism the "Great Vehicle" tradition, which includes both Zen and Tibetan Buddhism and stresses seeking enlightenment for all beings

meditation cultivation of skillful qualities of mind, particularly mindfulness

mental discipline teachings the Eightfold Path steps of wise effort, wise mindfulness, and wise concentration

metta (in Pali; *maitri* in Sanskrit) "lovingkindness" "friendliness," "benevolence"; often used as the object of a meditation practice

Middle Path balanced practice of mind and of body advocated by the Buddha; the path that avoids excessive sensual indulgence and excessive asceticism

mindfulness presence of mind or attentiveness to the present without "wobbling" or drifting away from experience

morality teachings the Eightfold Path steps of wise speech, wise action, and wise livelihood

nirvana (Sanskrit; *nibbana* in Pali) literally "blown out" or "extinguished"; liberation through enlightenment from the grasping or clinging that is the source of all suffering and to the rooting out of greed, hatred, and delusion

not-self (*anatta* in Pali; *anatman* in Sanskrit) the absence of or emptiness of a separate, autonomous, unchanging self; the heart of the teachings on the twelve links of dependent origination and thus right understanding; emptiness (*shunyata* in Sanskrit; *sunnata* in Pali) is the central teaching of Mahayana Buddhism

Precepts Buddhist guidelines for living a life of nonharming. For laypeople, the **Five Precepts** of Theravada Buddhism are to refrain from taking life, from taking what is not given, from false speech, from sexual misconduct, and from losing balance through taking intoxicants.

Refuges *See* Three Refuges

Sangha (Sanskrit) when capitalized, the Buddha's original community of disciples living under quite specific guidelines, but now expanded to include novitiates, lay practitioners, and sometimes all who follow a Buddhist spiritual path

Second Noble Truth the cause of *dukkha* (suffering) is grasping, greed, and the desire for things to be different than they are

Siddhartha Gautama (Sanskrit; Siddhatta Gotama in Pali) the given name of the historical Buddha

skillful means actions that lead to happiness, freedom, and awakening and that do not cause harm

sympathetic joy (*mudita* in Pali) taking delight in our own and others' successes

Theravada Buddhism the "Teaching of the Elders," the oldest tradition, which exists in the West primarily as Insight Meditation or Vipassana; considered by some to be the most traditional stream of Buddhist teachings

Third Noble Truth the end of *dukkha* is letting go of the craving that causes it; the possibility of enlightenment

Three Refuges Taking refuge in the Buddha (or our potential to awaken) / Taking refuge in the Dharma (or the path that awakens) / Taking refuge in the Sangha (or the community that practices this path); originally used as an expression of commitment to becoming a disciple of the Buddha; usually called Three Jewels or Three Treasures in Mahayana Buddhism

unskillful means actions that cause harm and lead to suffering

Vipassana (Pali for "insight meditation") the stream in Theravada Buddhism also known in the West as Insight Meditation

wisdom seeing what is skillful, appropriate, and timely

wisdom teachings the Eightfold Path steps of wise understanding (or wise view) and wise thought (or wise intention)

wise action the third step of the Eightfold Path: refraining from taking life, from taking what is not given, from sexual misconduct; living according to the Precepts

wise concentration the eighth step of the Eightfold Path; developing one-pointedness and skillful absorption for insight and enlightenment; meditation

wise effort the sixth step of the Eightfold Path; rousing will, making effort, exerting the mind, and striving, first, to prevent the arising and maintenance of unskillful states and, second, to awaken, enhance, and maintain skillful states "to the full perfection of development"; continually striving for mindfulness, especially in meditation

wise livelihood the fifth step of the Eightfold Path; supporting ourselves through work that is legal and peaceful and entails no harm to others—specifically, not to trade in arms or lethal weapons, intoxicants, or poisons or to kill animals

wise mindfulness the seventh step of the Eightfold Path; cultivating awareness of body, feelings, mental qualities, and mind objects

wise speech the third step of the Eightfold Path; abstaining from false, malicious, and harsh speech and idle chatter; determining whether the time for speech is appropriate and whether it is both useful and truthful; speaking in a way that causes no harm

wise thought or wise intention, resolve, aspiration, or motive; the second step of the Eightfold Path; renouncing ill will and cultivating skillful intentions; becoming aware of our thinking process; renouncing negative patterns of thought; and cultivating good will

wise understanding or wise view; the first step of the Eightfold Path; a thorough understanding of the Four Noble Truths, impermanence, *karma*, and not-self

APPENDIX: TWELVE STEPS AND TWELVE TRADITIONS

TWELVE STEPS

1. We admitted we were powerless over alcohol—that our lives had become unmanageable.
2. Came to believe that a Power greater than ourselves could restore us to sanity.
3. Made a decision to turn our will and our lives over to the care of God *as we understood Him.*
4. Made a searching and fearless moral inventory of ourselves.
5. Admitted to God, to ourselves, and to another human being the exact nature of our wrongs.

6. Were entirely ready to have God remove all these defects of character.

7. Humbly asked Him to remove our shortcomings.

8. Made a list of all persons we had harmed, and became willing to make amends to them all.

9. Made direct amends to such people wherever possible, except when to do so would injure them or others.

10. Continued to take personal inventory and when we were wrong promptly admitted it.

11. Sought through prayer and meditation to improve our conscious contact with God *as we understood Him*, praying only for knowledge of His will for us and the power to carry that out.

12. Having had a spiritual awakening as the result of these steps, we tried to carry this message to alcoholics, and to practice these principles in all our affairs.

TWELVE TRADITIONS

1. Our common welfare should come first; personal recovery depends upon AA unity.

2. For our group purpose there is but one ultimate authority—a loving God as He may express Himself in our group conscience. Our leaders are but trusted servants; they do not govern.

3. The only requirement for AA membership is a desire to stop drinking.

4. Each group should be autonomous except in matters affecting other groups or AA as a whole.

5. Each group has but one primary purpose—to carry its message to the alcoholic who still suffers.

6. An AA group ought never endorse, finance, or lend the AA name to any related facility or outside enterprise, lest problems of money, property, and prestige divert us from our primary purpose.

7. Every AA group ought to be fully self-supporting, declining outside contributions.

8. Alcoholics Anonymous should remain forever non-professional, but our service centers may employ special workers.

9. AA, as such, ought never be organized; but we may create service boards or committees directly responsible to those they serve.

10. Alcoholics Anonymous has no opinion on outside issues; hence the AA name ought never be drawn into public controversy.

11. Our public relations policy is based on attraction rather than promotion; we need always maintain personal anonymity at the level of press, radio, and films.

12. Anonymity is the spiritual foundation of all our traditions, ever reminding us to place principles before personalities.

Twelve Steps and Twelve Traditions. New York: The AA Grapevine, Inc., and Alcoholics Anonymous World Services, Inc., 1952.

INDEX

Dr. Bob S. *See* cofounders of AA
dukkha (suffering), xviii, 53, 55,
56, 59, 62–68, 72–74, 83–90,
97, 110, 111, 128, 133, 154,
159, 160, 166, 167, 169, 170

effort, 70, 76, 77, 80, 105, 120,
167, 168, 170. *See also* wise
effort
Eightfold Path, xvii, 53, 54, 69–
80, 110–24, 167–71. *See also*
mental disciple teachings;
morality teachings; wisdom
teachings
electroconvulsive therapy, 4
emotions. *See* mental formations
emptiness. *See* not-self
enlightened beings, 53, 74, 92,
109, 166
equanimity, 142, 160, 161, 166,
167

faith, xvii, 38, 96–98, 126
fear, 18, 21–24, 32, 38, 49, 99,
136–38, 143, 159
feelings, 10, 32, 51, 57–58, 63,
64, 80, 85, 95, 103, 131, 133,
134, 143, 159, 165–67, 171. *See
also* mental formations
financial insecurity, 32, 38, 136–
38
First Noble Truth, 55–59, 61,
110, 161
Five Hindrances, 79–80, 103,
121–24, 148, 167
Five Precepts, 74–75, 115–18,
122, 169, 170

forgiveness, 45–48
form, material, 57–59, 64, 85, 89
Four Noble Truths, xii, xvi, 53,
54, 6, 70, 83–84, 89–90, 93,
100, 130, 160, 167, 171. *See
also* First Noble Truth; Second
Noble Truth; Third Noble
Truth; Fourth Noble Truth;
Four Sober Truths
Four Sober Truths, 83–90
Fourth Noble Truth, xii, 53–54,
63, 68, 70–80, 167. *See also*
Eightfold Path
fourth step. *See* Step Four
freedom, 32–34, 38, 62, 69, 93,
127–29, 150, 151, 154, 167,
169

generosity, 114, 117, 150, 156,
157
genetic predisposition to alcoholism, 84
geographic cure, 88, 154
God, 5–7, 15–17, 19, 20, 27, 32,
36, 58, 92, 96, 97, 99, 100, 104,
140, 172, 173. *See also* Higher
Power
Goldstein, Joseph, 48, 59, 162
gossip, 72, 73, 113, 122. *See also*
wise speech
grasping, 59, 63–65, 127, 167, 169.
See also attachment; clinging
gratitude, 17, 21, 29, 34, 96
greed, 73, 74, 77, 97, 127, 152,
167, 169. *See also* desire; craving
Group of Drunks. *See* Higher
Power

HALT (Hungry-Angry-Lonely-Tired), 121–23
happiness, xii, 29, 32–34, 53, 69, 73, 76, 93, 111, 127–28, 150, 151, 154, 158, 159, 161, 169
helping professions, 118–19
Higher Power, 5, 12, 16, 17, 21–22, 24, 38, 89, 96, 104–05, 121, 140. *See also* God
hindrances. *See* Five Hindrances
home group (AA), 17, 20, 47
householders, 74, 98
humility, xix, 21, 22, 37

ignorance, 63, 85, 94, 152, 166
illness, as *dukkha*, 53, 61, 128
impermanence, 23, 73, 80, 93, 98, 100, 110, 111, 130, 134, 137, 140, 159, 160, 167, 171
Indra's net, 135
insanity of drinking, 16
insight (*vipassana*), 23, 48–49, 54, 71–72, 77, 80, 97, 99, 100, 104, 105, 118, 120, 122, 130, 138–39, 140, 168
Insight Meditation (Vipassana), 48, 102, 130, 140, 168, 170
intentionality, xviii, 47, 68, 70–71, 74, 76, 77, 95, 99–101, 104, 112–14, 120, 146–47, 152, 154, 157, 159, 168, 170, 171
interconnectedness, of life, 30, 73, 93, 114, 119, 135–37, 146, 152, 156
interrelationship. *See* interconnectedness
intoxicants, misuse of, 75, 118,

169, 171. *See also* alcoholism
inventory, taking one's, 18–19, 21, 26–27, 36–37, 49, 99–100, 102–4, 129–30. *See also* Step Four

job problems, 88, 127, 137–38. *See also* wise livelihood

kalyanamitta (spiritual friend), 150
karma, xvi, 67–68, 70, 73, 76, 87–89, 93, 95–98, 100–2, 110, 111, 121, 124, 129–30, 139, 152, 160, 168, 171
karma, law of, xviii, 93, 95
kindness, xi, 45, 68, 73, 89, 117. *See also* lovingkindness
Kornfield, Jack, 99, 164

labor malpractices, 74. *See also* wise livelihood
livelihood. *See* wise livelihood
lovingkindness (*metta*), 26, 142–155, 157, 159, 166, 168

meditation, xi, 16, 23, 27, 37, 46–50. *See also* mental discipline teachings
meditation instructions, 78
membership in AA, 92, 173
mental discipline teachings, 70, 76–79, 110–13, 168
mental formations, 57–59, 63, 70, 85, 165, 166
mental obsession, with alcohol, 61, 62, 84

metta. See lovingkindness

Middle Path, in Buddhism, 53, 168

Middle-Length Discourses of the Buddha (Majjhima Nikaya), 61, 164

mindfulness, 23, 48, 70, 75–77, 97, 100, 101, 104, 110, 120–21, 130, 140, 165, 167, 168, 171. *See also* meditation; mental discipline teachings

monkey mind, 103

morality teachings, 54, 69–70, 72–76, 110, 113–19, 168

motorcycle clubs, sober, 34

Nhat Hanh, Thich, 46–47, 164

natural resources, misuse of, 74

near enemy, 155

nibbana. See nirvana

Niebuhr, Reinhold, 36

nirvana, 63–63, 127, 167, 168

nonharming, 45, 48, 71, 72, 74–76, 97–99, 104, 106, 112, 115–20, 138, 139, 169. *See also* Five Precepts

noting, in meditation, 133–34

not-self (*anatta*), 56–59, 63, 70, 93, 94, 98, 99, 110, 111, 131, 140, 160, 169, 171

perception, 57–58, 64, 165

periodic drinker, 8

physical compulsion to drink, 61, 86, 87

powerlessness, over alcohol, 14, 36, 96. *See also* Step One

prayer, 16, 17, 27, 36, 37, 80, 99, 104, 130, 143, 160

precepts. *See* Five Precepts

prejudice, 73

present moment, being in, 18, 26, 62, 76, 97, 113, 120–21, 130, 134, 136, 145, 149

prisons, AA meetings in, 48–50

promises, in AA, and in Buddhism, 31–39, 125–41

re-action, 129

recovery, from alcoholism, xvi–xix, 12, 19, 31–39, 95–97, 111, 113, 114, 119, 123, 135, 137, 147, 148, 158, 173

religion and spirituality, 7–8

renunciation, 71, 112

resentments, 112–13, 122, 145, 146

responsibility pledge, AA, 116–17

restlessness, 80, 103, 122–27, 167. *See also* Five Hindrances

Salzberg, Sharon, 68, 164

sangha, 92–93, 101, 169, 170. *See also* Three Refuges

Second Noble Truth, xii, 56, 60–61, 110, 159, 169

Seeking the Heart of Wisdom (Goldstein and Kornfield), 48, 264

self, concept of. *See* not-self

self-centered fear, 22, 24

selfing, 124, 131–36, 158

sense gates/organs, 57, 58, 63, 64, 66, 85, 86, 165, 166

WHAT TO READ NEXT FROM WISDOM PUBLICATIONS

Let Go
A Buddhist Guide to Breaking Free of Habits
Martine Batchelor

"A marvelous guide to a habit-free life."—*Mandala*

Mindfulness in Plain English
Bhante Gunaratana

"A masterpiece."—Jon Kabat-Zinn

Life Is Spiritual Practice
Achieving Happiness with the Ten Perfections
Jean Smith

"An accessible and down-to-earth commentary on Buddha's teachings of the 10 Perfections."—*Spirituality & Practice*

About Wisdom Publications

Wisdom Publications is the leading publisher of classic and contemporary Buddhist books and practical works on mindfulness. To learn more about us or to explore our other books, please visit our website at wisdomexperience.org or contact us at the address below.

Wisdom Publications
199 Elm Street
Somerville, MA 02144 USA

We are a 501(c)(3) organization, and donations in support of our mission are tax deductible.

Wisdom Publications is affiliated with the Foundation for the Preservation of the Mahayana Tradition (FPMT).